standard
grade
study-mate

geography

second edition

Calvin Clarke

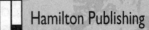
Hamilton Publishing

a handbook of key facts, practice questions and practical advice

standard
grade
study-mate

geography

(second edition)

First Published 1994
Second Edition 2000
© Calvin Clarke 1994, 2000
ISBN 0 946164 38 X   2nd edition
(ISBN 0 946164 23 1   1st edition)

*A catalogue record for this book is available from
the British Library.*

Orders can be made *direct* over the phone
Contact Thomson Litho, Hamilton Publishing (Sales)
on (01355) 233081

Access and Visa Cards accepted

Letter accepted with school or personal cheque

Cover design Smith & Paul Design Associates, Paisley

Published by
Hamilton Publishing
A division of M & A Thomson Litho Limited
10–16 Colvilles Place, Kelvin Industrial Estate,
EAST KILBRIDE G75 0SN

Printed and bound in Great Britain by
M & A Thomson Litho Ltd., East Kilbride, Scotland

CONTENTS

BsB £1·95
D3   2

INTRODUCTION

This *Standard Grade Study-Mate* for Geography is designed as a supplement to your Geography coursework. It concentrates on building up the skills you need to tackle examination-style questions by giving examples of the different types of questions together with advice about how to approach them.

This book does not attempt to give the detailed content of the whole Standard Grade syllabus, but it does summarise the essential elements of every topic within the course.

CC 2000

ACKNOWLEDGEMENTS

The Author and Publisher would like to thank the following for permission to reproduce copyright material in this book:

Aerofilms Limited for photographs on pages 46 and 66;

The Controller of Her Majesty's Stationery Office for Crown Copyright Map material reproduced from 1989 Ordnance Survey 1:50 000 Second Series on page 40, and map extracts on page 65;

Lothian and Edinburgh Enterprise Limited for the advertisement on page 7;

The Scottish Qualifications Authority for illustrations on pages 3, 51 (Reference Diagram Q3), 54, 84 and 97 (Reference Diagram Q1A).

CHAPTER ONE

THE STANDARD GRADE GEOGRAPHY EXAMINATIONS

▶ THE GRADES AWARDED

Candidates sitting Standard Grade Geography receive an award from grades 1 – 7.

Grade 1 ⎫
Grade 2 ⎬ **Credit Level**

Grade 3 ⎫
Grade 4 ⎬ **General Level**

Grade 5 ⎫
Grade 6 ⎬ **Foundation Level**

Grade 7   **Course Completed**

▶ THE ELEMENTS OF THE COURSE

The overall award is calculated from the grades awarded for the two different elements of the course, which are:

Knowledge and Understanding

Enquiry Skills

The *Knowledge and Understanding* element carries a weighting of 40%. The *Enquiry Skills* are worth 60%. If a candidate achieves a grade 1 for *Knowledge and Understanding* but a grade 2 for *Enquiry*, his overall grade is a grade 2 because the *Enquiry Skills* carry a greater weighting than does the *Knowledge and Understanding*. Both of these elements are assessed by means of external SQA examinations at the end of the course.

▶ THE EXAMINATION PAPERS

The *Knowledge and Understanding* and the *Enquiry* elements are assessed when the candidates sit two of the following papers:

Foundation Paper for grades 5 and 6   lasts 1 hr. 5 mins.
General Paper   for grades 3 and 4   lasts 1 hr. 25 mins.
Credit Paper   for grades 1 and 2   lasts 2 hrs.

To achieve the higher of the two grades at each level, the candidate must score approximately 70 per cent in the examination. To achieve the lower grade, approximately 45 per cent must be scored.

While it is not possible for each question paper to contain questions on every topic within the syllabus, a wide variety of topics are tested and a range of question types are set. There will be at least one map-based question in each paper.

Candidates must answer all the questions in the examination papers.

▶ SITTING THE EXAMINATION

EQUIPMENT

You should take a pen, a spare pen, a pencil, a pencil sharpener, a rubber, a ruler, and liquid paper into the examination. You may possibly need a calculator although any arithmetic you have to do should be quite simple.

You should think carefully about using liquid paper. Many candidates use it to erase mistakes, but then forget to put in the correct word after it has dried. This could cost you marks. There is nothing wrong with crossing out wrong words or even whole paragraphs in an examination. As long as your answer is legible, you will not be penalised for being untidy.

TIMING

One of the biggest problems for candidates sitting Standard Grade is timing. It is difficult to know whether you are answering questions at the right pace when there are so many questions and some questions can be longer than others.

As a rule, Credit Papers have questions totalling approximately 80 marks, which have to be completed in 2 hours or 120 minutes. This means you have, on average, $1\frac{1}{2}$ minutes for each mark. The General Paper has questions totalling approximately 70 marks and lasts for 85 minutes, giving just over one minute per mark. However, this method of judging pace is probably too complicated to be of use in the middle of an important examination. A quicker way might be to work out where you should be half-way through your allocated time. You could divide the number of questions by two. So, if there are eight questions in the Credit Paper, you should have completed question 4 after one hour. Or, for a Credit Paper, you could count up the first 40 marks and that will be approximately half-way through. For a General Paper half-way is after the first 35 marks approximately, which should take you 40 minutes.

By checking your pace, you will find out whether you are going too slowly and will have to speed up. On the other hand, you might find that you are going too fast. It is a reasonable assumption that, if you are well ahead of time, either you are a genius or your answers are not as complete as they need to be. Remember also that every paper has several map-based questions and candidates usually find that these take a little longer to answer.

ANSWERING THE QUESTIONS

Read the whole of a question before beginning your answer and look at all the reference diagrams and maps shown. All of them are clearly named. Reference Diagram Q1 refers to question 1, Reference Diagram Q2 is for question 2, and so on.

You may find that it helps to write brief notes on the question paper or answer paper before you begin to write your complete answer. This is perfectly acceptable, but if you write notes on your answer paper, be sure to cross them out before writing your proper answer.

If you encounter questions for which you cannot think of an answer or a full answer, write whatever notes you can on it and then leave it until later. By that time you may have thought of other relevant points to make.

AT THE END OF THE EXAMINATION

You will have been told many times to check your answers at the end of an examination. Concentrate on these areas:
1 For questions that ask you to make a choice, make sure that you have given your choice clearly and not just the reasons for your choice.
2 Check the 'describe' questions and the 'explain' questions. Have you answered these correctly?
3 For mapwork questions, have you given grid references for the locations you have referred to on the map?
4 If there is still time left, try and add more details to your answers, especially those worth a lot of marks. You can always continue your answers at the end of the examination paper.

CHAPTER TWO
TYPES OF EXAMINATION QUESTIONS

INTRODUCTION

The people who make up Standard Grade Geography examinations can choose from a wide variety of questions. But they must ask certain types of questions, and these questions must relate to the topics which are in the syllabus.

The types of questions fall into two main categories (called **elements**) – those which test your knowledge and understanding of the syllabus (**Knowledge and Understanding questions**) and those which test your ability to use these facts and ideas to solve geographical problems (**Enquiry questions**).

You will be awarded separate marks for your answers to the questions in each element and you will be awarded separate grades for them on your certificate.

By looking at the right-hand side of each page of the examination paper, you can see which element each question tests. The Knowledge and Understanding column is on the left and the Enquiry column on the right. The element tested in each question is shown by a line across its column, opposite the number of marks awarded. For example, in the diagram below the question is testing Knowledge and Understanding.

	KU	ES
Marks		
6. (*a*) Explain what is meant by the term 'International Aid'.		
(2)		

There are three main types of Knowledge and Understanding questions and five main types of Enquiry questions, but they do not appear in any order in the examination.

A Knowledge and Understanding question could be followed by one type of Enquiry question and then by another type of Enquiry question.

All the main types of questions will now be considered. Examples of each will be given, together with advice on how you should tackle them.

Following this, there is a section on mapwork questions, as these need special attention.

KNOWLEDGE AND UNDERSTANDING QUESTIONS

▶ **1   SELECTING, DESCRIBING, PROVIDING EXAMPLES**

These questions ask you either to select the correct answer from a list of choices, or to describe an aspect of the syllabus, or to provide examples of a part of the syllabus.

QUESTION PHRASING

The questions are often phrased in the following ways:

Match the features in the diagram to their correct names.

Which of the above is an example of . . .?

Match the land use descriptions to the grid references.

Describe the physical features of . . ..

Describe the economic consequences of . . ..

Name features A, B and C.

Name four elements of the weather.

Name four glacial landforms shown on the diagram.

Give two pieces of evidence that show that . . ..

POINTS TO BEAR IN MIND

1   Many of the questions will have a resource, e.g. a map or a diagram. Such questions will begin **Look at Reference Diagram Q....** Make sure you read this instruction and find the correct resource. It will provide you with the information you need to answer the question.

2   Some of the questions ask you to **describe**. This means that you just state the main points or characteristics. You do **not** need to give any reasons.

3   Look out for the key nouns (e.g. landform, weather element) and adjectives (e.g. social, environmental, physical, urban) which tell you exactly what you should be writing about. The meanings of these key words are found in the Vocabulary sections of Chapter 3.

GENERAL LEVEL QUESTIONS

1   *Reference Diagram Q1: Stages in desert expansion*

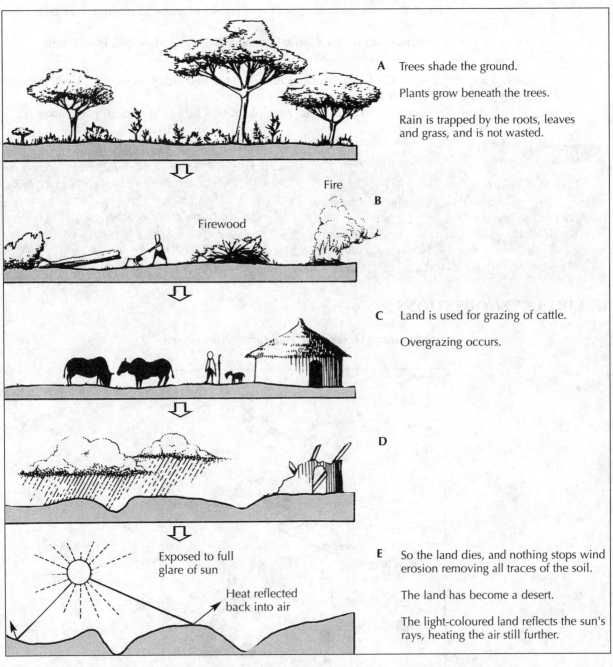

A Trees shade the ground.

Plants grow beneath the trees.

Rain is trapped by the roots, leaves and grass, and is not wasted.

Fire

B

Firewood

C Land is used for grazing of cattle.

Overgrazing occurs.

D

Exposed to full glare of sun

Heat reflected back into air

E So the land dies, and nothing stops wind erosion removing all traces of the soil.

The land has become a desert.

The light-coloured land reflects the sun's rays, heating the air still further.

Look at Reference Diagram Q1 which shows the ways by which deserts expand.
Describe stages B and D.   (4)

ADVICE

(a) **Check the number of marks.** There are two marks awarded for each stage, so write down two points or a developed point: e.g. for stage B, *'The trees are cut down'* is worth only 1 mark. A developed point, *'The trees are cut down to make farmland and provide firewood'*, is worth 2 marks.

(b) **Choose the most relevant answer.** For example, in stage D, *'the house is falling down'* is probably not worth a mark, because it is not a stage in the expansion of the desert. It would be better to write *'People are moving away and the houses are abandoned'*, which would be worth 1 mark. But the most relevant answer would describe the heavy rain eroding the soil, making gullies and making it impossible to farm.

5

2   *Reference Table Q2: International aid schemes*

> 1 MALAYSIA: Britain supplies drinking water schemes in Malaysia, the goods and services being supplied by British companies.
> 2 CAMBODIA: Oxfam provides water supplies for villages in Cambodia, from money raised in Britain.
> 3 IRAN: Iran exchanges crude oil for £140 million worth of car parts with a British firm.

Look at Reference Table Q2 above. Much of British aid is **tied aid**. This means it has to be used to buy goods or services from Britain.
(a) Which of the schemes in the table is an example of tied aid?   (b) Explain your choice. (2)

CREDIT LEVEL QUESTIONS

3   *Reference Map Q3: Weather map for 30 November 1977*

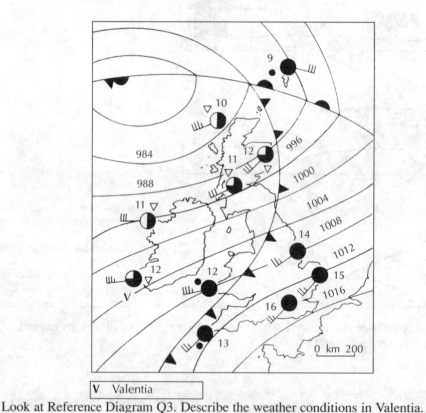

> **V**   Valentia

Look at Reference Diagram Q3. Describe the weather conditions in Valentia.   (3)

WITH A BUSINESS DEVELOPMENT SITE OF THE QUALITY OF WEST LOTHIAN'S STARLAW PARK, YOU'LL HAVE TO GET IN THERE QUICK.

Starlaw Park is one of the finest business development sites anywhere in Britain.

This is not just a mere assertion. Already inter-national companies such as Mitsubishi, NEC, Motorola, and Ethicon are in the area. Here are just a few of the reasons why you too could be enjoying possibly the shrewdest business move you'll ever make;

| An attractive countryside setting.

| A strategic location on the edge of Livingston New Town, close to the M8. Fast access to both Edinburgh and Glasgow, and to the two cities' international airports.

| A dedicated motorway junction and a new trunk road through the site.

| Plans underway for a filling station, hotel and restaurant. Business Park composed of 56 acre north site and 20 acre south site.

| Site servicing well underway, with a spur road into the north site and first phase landscaping due for completion in Spring '93.

| A highly skilled and educated local labour pool, and a number of major universities and colleges within easy reach.

| A full support service is available from Lothian and Edinburgh Enterprise Limited.

So, stake the best claim you'll ever make.

Phone Lothian and Edinburgh Enterprise Limited Business Property Dept. on 0131-313 4000 (24 hrs), and ask for details on Starlaw Park.

Lothian and Edinburgh Enterprise Limited

Look at Reference Diagram Q4. It shows an advertisement to attract industry to the former Lothian Region.

Name **three** factors mentioned in the advertisement which influence the location of manufacturing industry.

(3)

(a) **Answer the question directly.** The key word is 'factor'. So 'Good road communications' is a better answer than 'close to the M8'.

(b) **Beware of red herrings.** A filling station, hotel and restaurant are very borderline as factors and best avoided when there are more obvious answers.

▶ 2 EXPLAINING

These questions are chosen to test how well you understand the ideas in the syllabus. They are the most common types of question in the examination.

QUESTION PHRASING

The questions ask you to give reasons, but they may be phrased in different ways, e.g.

Give reasons why . . . .

Explain why . . . .

Account for the differences between . . . .

Suggest why . . . .

Explain the changes . . . .

POINTS TO BEAR IN MIND

1 This type of question is often badly answered by candidates in examinations as they confuse the words 'describe' and 'explain'. For any question which asks you to explain **you must give reasons**. Describing will earn you no marks.

2 The reasons you give should be thorough and clearly stated. You can often earn more than one mark for each point you make by providing a detailed or developed reason.

3 Because these questions test your understanding of the syllabus, there may not be a resource diagram to accompany the question. In some questions, however, diagrams are provided to 'cue you in'. Make sure you read all the information in these resources as they may provide clues to the answers needed.

4 Some of the questions may ask you to give an exact number of reasons. If you can give more reasons than asked for, without using up valuable time, do so – just in case one of your first answers is incorrect.

5 Other questions may just ask you to 'suggest why' or 'explain' and not tell you how many reasons to give. For these questions also write as many reasons as you can, making sure you explain each point thoroughly.

1   *Reference Map Q1: Migration from North Africa to France in the 1980s*

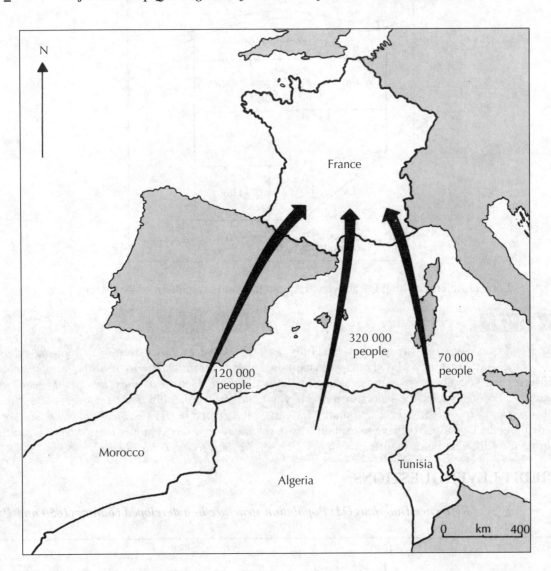

Look at Reference Map Q1.

Give **two** reasons why people leave developing countries such as Algeria to live in developed countries such as France. (4)

(a) **Do not be put off** if you have not studied migration to France. The question just uses France and Algeria as examples, but it asks you to write about migration from developing countries in general. As long as you have studied migration from any developing country and can remember the reasons why people move away, you can answer this question.

(b) **Look at the marks.** You are asked to give two reasons and yet the total mark is four. So each reason is worth two marks, and to deserve both marks it must be very detailed. Reasons such as '*For a job*' or '*Poor farming*' or '*For more money*' would

certainly not receive two marks. Instead of '*Poor farming*' you could write '*Poor farming in developing countries caused by infertile soils and an unreliable climate*' or '*Poor farming in developing countries which results in farmers having little money to improve their farms*'.

(c) **Beware of generalised answers** such as '*For a higher standard of living*'. It would earn you more marks to write '*For a greater opportunity to enjoy better medical care, more education, improved housing and superior working conditions*'. This answer means the same as a higher standard of living, but by breaking it down into four parts, it is worth more marks.

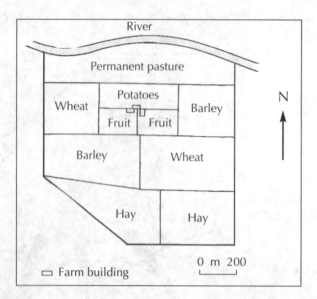

Look at Reference Map Q2 above.   Explain the land use pattern on Netherlaw Farm. (2)

ADVICE

(a) **Read every word in the question carefully**, as two of the words are crucial. Firstly the word **explain** tells you that you must give reasons and not merely describe. Secondly it is the land use **pattern** you must explain. You would receive no marks for just explaining the land use. You have to explain why the farmer uses different fields in different ways.

(b) **Give exact answers**. *'So that the crops which need most attention are near the farmhouse'* could be improved to *'Potatoes and fruit need a lot of attention and are grown close to the farmhouse. Wheat and barley need less attention and are further away, and hay requires least attention and is found furthest from the farmhouse'*.

CREDIT LEVEL QUESTIONS

3   *Reference Diagrams Q3: Population structure in a developed country (1850 and 1990)*

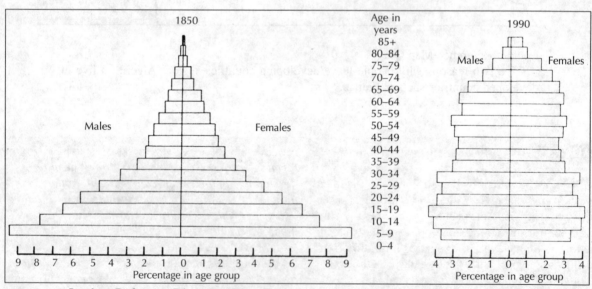

Look at Reference Diagrams Q3.   Explain the changes in the birth-rates and death-rates of a typical developed country between 1850 and 1990.   (6)

ADVICE

Structure your answer. Write down all the reasons for the lower birth-rate first, and then the reasons for the lower death-rate. This should make your answer much clearer.

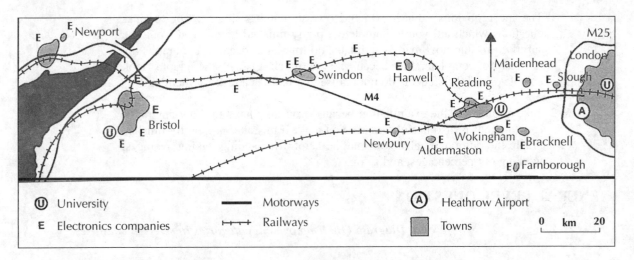

Look at Reference Map Q4.

Many electronics companies have located in the M4 corridor because of:

(a) the good communications

(b) nearby universities

(c) the availability of science parks.

Choose one of these three factors and explain its importance to an electronics company.   (3)

ADVICE

(a) **Do not be put off** if you have not studied the M4 corridor. As long as you understand the location of factories, you can answer this question.

(b) **Make the most suitable selection,** by choosing the factor you have most to write about. If you think one of the choices is easy and can be answered in one short sentence, it probably means you do not know enough about it to earn the three marks, and you should choose one of the others instead.

(c) **Beware of giving 'ghost' reasons** – answers which are not reasons at all, e.g. *'It is important for an electronics company to have good communications as they need to be near main roads and airports'*. This is not a reason. It is just a rephrasing of the first part of the sentence. Similarly, *'Good communications allow transport to and from the factory'* is not much better. Neither answer attempts to give reasons why it is important for the companies to be beside fast roads and near airports.

▶ 3   DRAWING AND UNDERSTANDING DIAGRAMS

This type of question tests your skills in drawing and reading different kinds of diagrams. The diagrams might be graphs, tables or charts. Those that occur most frequently in the examination are line graphs, bar graphs, pie-graphs, cross-sections, population pyramids and flow-line maps.

QUESTION PHRASING

These questions ask you

either (a) to draw/complete diagrams.
             e.g. Complete the graph above . . . .
             Draw another type of graph to show the information . . . .
             Mark on the cross-section the location of . . . .

or   (b) to read information from diagrams.
             e.g. Describe the stages shown by the flow-line map . . . .
             Use the bar graphs to work out the fastest growing cities . . . .
             According to the pie-graph what percentage of the population work
             in . . . .

POINTS TO BEAR IN MIND

1 The most obvious advice, which is worth emphasising, is not to miss questions which tell you to complete a partly-finished graph. You would be surprised to find how many candidates do this – not because the graphs are difficult to complete, but because, at a quick glance, the graphs look complete, and the students do not realise that there is a task for them to do.

2 Take a ruler into the examination because you may have to draw diagrams. Liquid paper is also useful, in case you make a mistake on a partly-finished graph. In addition, a calculator may be helpful for adding, taking averages, working out percentages, and so on.

GENERAL LEVEL QUESTIONS

1   *Reference Diagram Q1: Employment categories in selected countries*

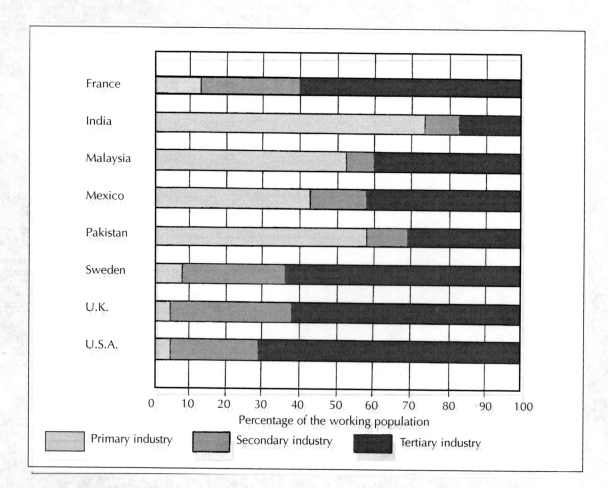

Look at the Reference Diagram Q1 above.

    Which of the countries have more than 20 per cent of their working population in secondary industry?   (2)

12

Reference Diagram Q2: Population of Egypt

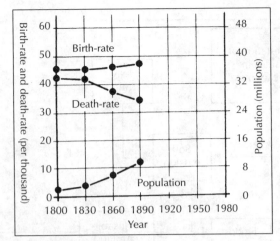

Look at Reference Diagram Q2 above.
Complete the graph using the information below. (3)

Population characteristics of Egypt			
	1920	*1950*	*1980*
Birth-rate (per thousand)	46	45	38
Death-rate (per thousand)	29	45	13
Population (millions)	13	20	42

CREDIT LEVEL QUESTIONS

3   *Reference Diagram Q3*

Country	Gross domestic product per capita	Death-rate (per thousand)
Niger	$ 750	24
Mozambique	$ 810	18
Cuba	$3000	6
Egypt	$3820	9
Mexico	$6400	5

Draw a diagram or diagrams to show clearly the relationship between the gross domestic product per capita and the death-rate for the five countries shown in Reference Diagram Q3. (4)

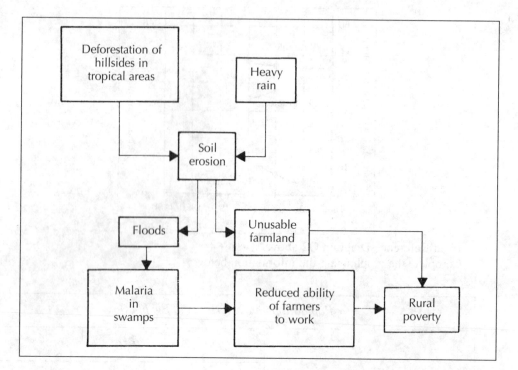

Describe the effects of deforestation of hillsides in tropical areas as shown by Reference Diagram Q4.

(4)

ADVICE

(a) **Think your answer through before** you begin to write. Your answer could become very confused unless you take the correct approach. Always start with the first stage. Do not be tempted to begin with *'The poverty of the rural areas is due to . . .'.*

(b) **Avoid long sentences.** A series of short sentences is much clearer, e.g. *'Deforestation leads to soil erosion. Soil erosion makes land unusable for farming. This causes poverty. Soil erosion also causes floods . . .'.*

ENQUIRY QUESTIONS

▶ 1 INTERPRETING/DESCRIBING RELATIONSHIPS

This type of question also deals with diagrams although it may include text as well. The difference between these questions and those in the last section is that here you are expected to do more than just extract information from the diagrams. You must interpret them, in many cases bringing out the relationship between the information given in the different diagrams.

QUESTION PHRASING

These questions are often phrased as follows:

Describe the distribution of towns shown in . . . .
Describe the main features of the climate of . . . .
Compare the two diagrams . . . .
What are the main differences between . . . .
In what ways have variations in birth-rates and death-rates affected population growth?
Use the information in the diagram to explain why . . . .

POINTS TO BEAR IN MIND

1 These questions always have resources (diagrams, tables, text, etc). In many cases all the information you need in order to answer the question is provided. Your job is to sift through and extract the relevant items of information so that you can answer the question.

2 Do not rush. There is often a lot of information provided which you need to read through carefully. The time you spend doing this will be time well spent. It will save you time when you are composing your answer.

3 There are many key words used in these questions, e.g. *distribution, relationship, pattern*. Make sure you know their meanings. If you do not, you cannot possibly answer the question correctly.

GENERAL LEVEL QUESTIONS

1   *Reference Map Q1: Coal-fired power stations in the United Kingdom*

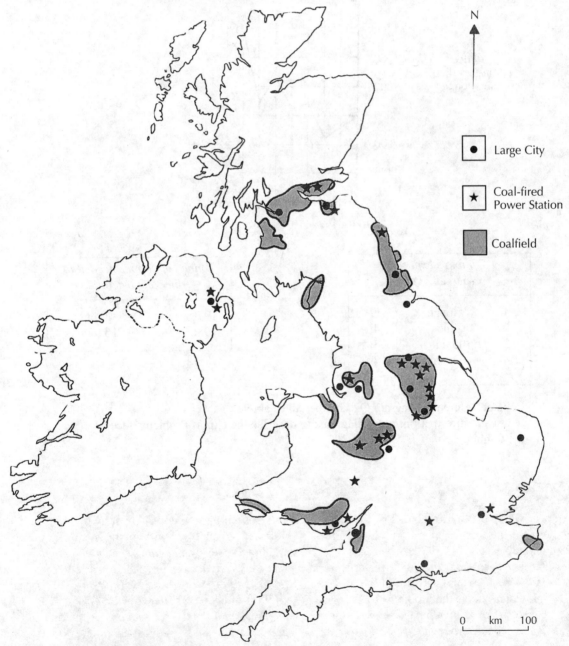

Look at Reference Map Q1.

Describe the distribution of coal-fired power stations in the United Kingdom.   (3)

(a) **Check the key words.** The question asks you to *describe*, not to give reasons. And you must write about the *distribution*, which is the spread of or pattern made by the power stations.

(b) **Give a detailed answer.** Do not look for a single phrase which describes where they are all found. Instead use phrases such as '*Most are found ...*', and '*There is a concentration ...*'.

(c) **Use directions** when describing the distribution, e.g. '*Most coal-fired power stations are found in central England and some are in South Wales, central Scotland and Northern Ireland*'.

(d) **Use all the information given** on the map, namely the cities and the coalfields. These must have been included for a reason. For example, you could write '*Most coal-fired power stations are on or near coalfields*' or '*Nearly all the coal-fired power stations are within 50 km of a large city*'.

2

Reference Diagram and Tables Q2

World price of copper (1970–86)

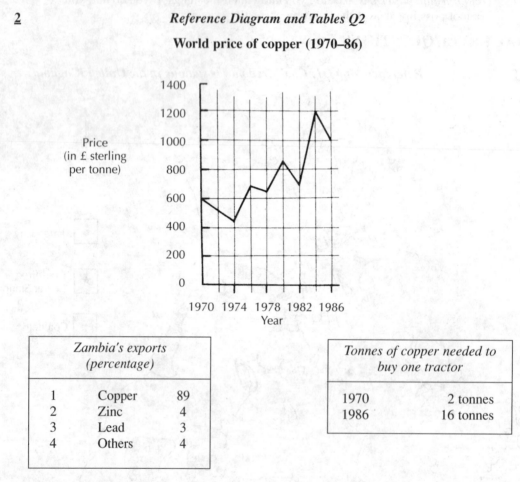

Zambia's exports (percentage)		
1	Copper	89
2	Zinc	4
3	Lead	3
4	Others	4

Tonnes of copper needed to buy one tractor	
1970	2 tonnes
1986	16 tonnes

Look at Reference Diagram Q2 and the tables above.
Use the information in the diagrams to describe the export problems faced by Zambia.

(3)

(a) **Answer the question directly.** It is not enough just to describe in sentences the information in the diagram and tables, e.g. '*In 1970, two tonnes of copper bought one tractor. In 1986 sixteen tonnes of copper were needed.*' You must sift out the information which shows the problems of Zambia's exports, e.g. '*In 1986 Zambia had to export eight times as much copper to buy one tractor as it did in 1970*'.

(b) **Describe the trends** shown by the figures. Do not get bogged down with giving lots of figures. For example, instead of saying '*The money Zambia received from its copper in 1970 was £600 per tonne, and in 1972 it was £550, and in 1974 it was £450...*', it is much better to write '*The money Zambia received from its copper varied greatly from year to year, reaching £1200 per tonne in 1984, but as low as £450 per tonne in 1974.*'

3   *Reference Diagrams Q3: Urban patterns in Coventry*

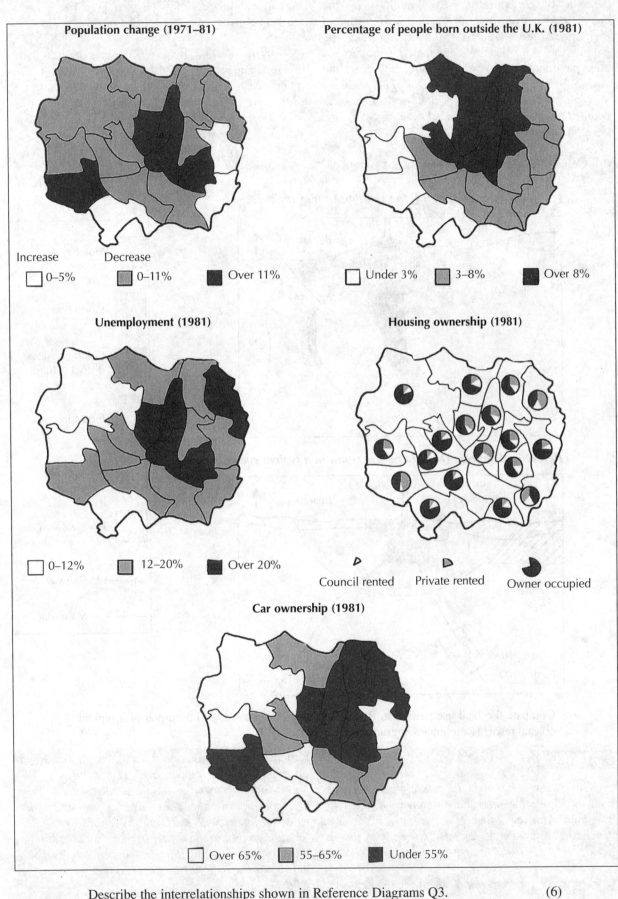

Population change (1971–81)

Increase   Decrease
☐ 0–5%   ◪ 0–11%   ■ Over 11%

Percentage of people born outside the U.K. (1981)

☐ Under 3%   ◪ 3–8%   ■ Over 8%

Unemployment (1981)

☐ 0–12%   ◪ 12–20%   ■ Over 20%

Housing ownership (1981)

Council rented   Private rented   Owner occupied

Car ownership (1981)

☐ Over 65%   ◪ 55–65%   ■ Under 55%

Describe the interrelationships shown in Reference Diagrams Q3.   (6)

4   *Reference Diagram Q4A: Land use zones in Ryde*

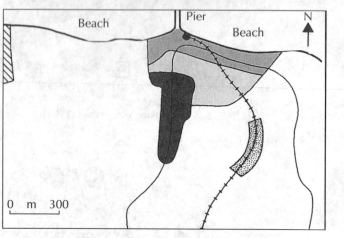

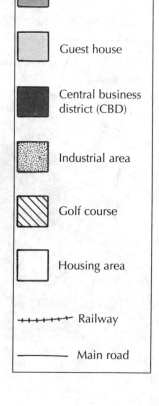

Reference Diagram Q4B: Land use zones in a typical coastal resort

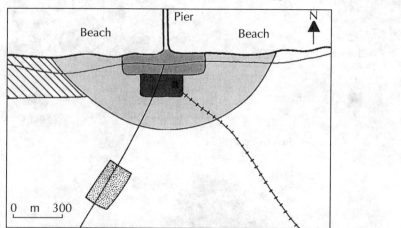

Compare the land use pattern in Ryde (Reference Diagram Q4A) with that of a typical coastal resort (Reference Diagram Q4B).   (6)

▶ 2 EVALUATING/CHOOSING

These questions ask you to evaluate or make an educated choice between two or more alternatives based on your understanding of geography. They may also ask you to consider the possible consequences of your choice, such as what effects it might have.

QUESTION PHRASING

These are some of the questions you will find:
Which is the best location (A, B or C) for a factory/New Town/superstore/by-pass?
Which land use is most appropriate in area X – an HEP station or a forest plantation or a reservoir?
Do you think the statement is fair/justified/accurate?

POINTS TO BEAR IN MIND

1 For most of these questions you do not receive any marks for the choice you make. This is because two or three of the choices might be acceptable. You earn your marks for giving valid geographical reasons for the choice you make.

2 Resources are always provided for these questions to help you make your choice and justify it.

GENERAL LEVEL QUESTIONS

<u>1</u>

Reference Diagram Q1A: Location factors for superstores

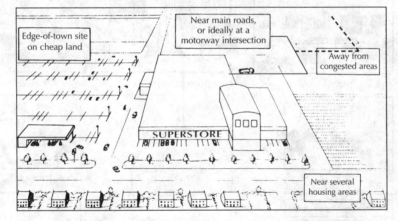

Reference Diagram Q1B: Possible locations for a superstore

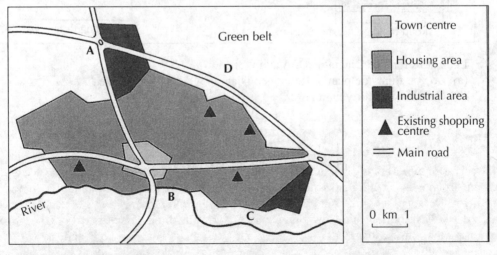

Look at Reference Diagrams Q1A and Q1B.
(a) Which of the four locations (A, B, C or D) in Reference Diagram Q1B would be the best for a new superstore?
(b) Give reasons for your answer.   (3)

ADVICE

(a) **Choose the most suitable site.** All the sites have advantages, but you should choose the one with the most advantages. This will mean that you will have more reasons to give – which will earn you more marks. Site A, despite being near an industrial area, has four advantages.

(b) **Negative reasons are acceptable.** As well as giving the advantages of your choice, it is acceptable to write down the disadvantages of the sites you have rejected.

(c) **Use all the information given.** For example, in Reference Diagram Q1B, the examiners have deliberately included other shopping centres. You should be able to work out that a new superstore would be best located away from existing shopping centres.

2   *Reference Diagram Q2A*

STOP BUYING GOODS MADE FROM
RAINFOREST TREES.
It is the best way of
saving the rainforests.

Reference Diagram Q2B: Reasons why rainforests are destroyed

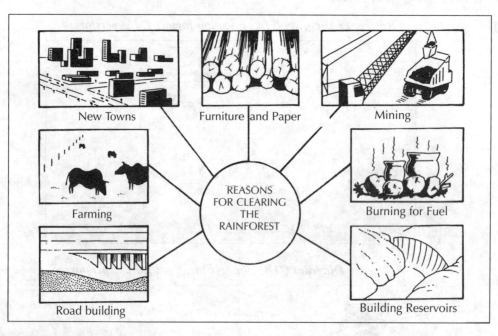

Look at Reference Diagrams Q2A and Q2B.
(a) Do you think the plan in Reference Diagram Q2A is a good idea?
(b) Give reasons for your answer.   (3)

ADVICE

(a) **Answer yes or no.** This is obvious, but crucial, advice. The examiners award marks according to how well your reasons support your view of the statement. If you have not given a view, you cannot earn any marks for your reasons.

(b) **Make as many points as possible** from the information given. For example, if you say *'Yes, it* *is a good idea, because if no-one bought these goods there would be no point in cutting down the trees for paper and furniture'*, this would earn two marks but not all three. Use more of the information in Reference Diagram Q2B and say *'In addition fewer roads would be needed and, with fewer jobs, not as many towns would be built. All this would save the rainforests from being destroyed.'*

20

CREDIT LEVEL QUESTIONS

3   *Reference Table Q3*

Types of aid	
Short-term aid	Supplies of grain, seeds and other foods.
Project aid	Money for one large dam and reservoir to provide irrigation water and hydro-electricity.
Non-project aid	Money for new wells in 50 villages with one worker in each village trained to give agricultural advice.

A developing country in Africa has been suffering from drought and food shortages for several years.

(a) Which of the three types of aid in Reference Table Q3 would be the most appropriate to give?

(b) Give detailed reasons for your answer. (4)

4   *Reference Text Q4:*   *Reference Map Q4:*
              The Golden Triangle   *Location of the Golden Triangle*

A company wishes to build a huge out-of-town centre, including shops, a hotel, cinemas and parking for 5,500 cars in the 'Golden Triangle' between the M1 and the M25. Three million people live within 30 minutes of this location, said to be the most accessible in Britain. The problem is that it lies in London's Green Belt.

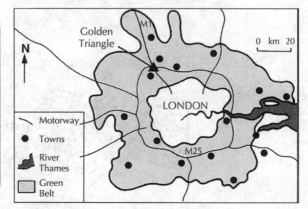

Look at the information in Reference Text Q4 and Reference Map Q4.

(a) Do you think that the development in London's Green Belt, described in Reference Text Q4, is justified?

(b) Give detailed reasons for your answer. (6)

These questions are concerned with geographical issues – developments which are controversial because some people think they are good ideas while others do not.

QUESTION PHRASING

The questions are often phrased as follows:

What are the arguments for and against a cement works being built at X?
Choose one type of urban redevelopment scheme, and describe its advantages and disadvantages.
Explain the different points of view people might have towards a new motorway/reservoir/factory.

POINTS TO BEAR IN MIND

1 You are expected to be able to look at an issue from all sides. You must think of all the different people who would be affected by a development: put yourself into their shoes and state what their opinions might be.

2 These answers may be quite lengthy. You may find it helpful to jot down rough notes first. You can do this at the start of each question and then cross them out before writing your answer. Alternatively you can use the margin, the pages at the end of the answer book or rough paper.

GENERAL LEVEL QUESTIONS

<u>1</u> *Reference Diagram Q1: Location of a quarry in North-West Scotland*

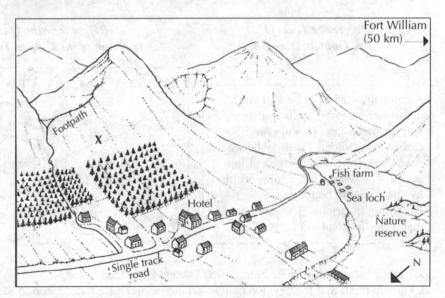

What are the arguments for and against setting up a quarry at place X in Reference Diagram Q1? (4)

ADVICE

(a) **Read the question carefully.** You have to give arguments for *and* against.

(b) **Avoid listing.** You should have little trouble in thinking of arguments, but do not write them all down as a list. A list is not just short statements written underneath each other. The following is also considered by the examiners to be a list: *'The arguments against the quarry are that it will spoil the* scenery, put off tourists, make noise, make dust, upset villagers, and spoil the nature reserve.' One way to avoid listing is to make sure that each sentence you write only concerns a single point.

(c) **Expand your answer.** This is the best way to avoid lists. Take each point and explain fully why it is an advantage or a disadvantage, e.g. *'The quarry will put off tourists, and this will mean less business for the hotels and less work for local people in the hotels.'*

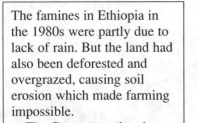

The famines in Ethiopia in the 1980s were partly due to lack of rain. But the land had also been deforested and overgrazed, causing soil erosion which made farming impossible.

The Government's scheme was to resettle 1.5 million people from the worst famine areas in the highlands to the lowlands further south. At the same time it began planting trees in the highlands.

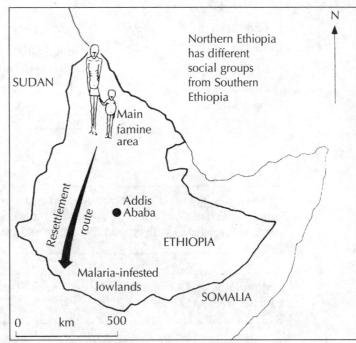

Look at Reference Text Q2 and Reference Map Q2.
Give one advantage and one disadvantage of the Ethiopian Government's scheme. (4)

ADVICE

(a) **Look at the number of marks.** Each advantage and each disadvantage earns two marks. So expand each point you make into a full explanation, e.g. *'One disadvantage is the threat of malaria to the people who would then be unable to work and produce enough food.'*

(b) **Think before you write.** Of all the views that could be given, choose the ones that you can explain in the greatest detail.

CREDIT LEVEL QUESTIONS

3   *Reference Texts Q3*

1973
The major oil-producing countries form an alliance called OPEC.

1974
Oil prices are four times as high as last year.

Look at Reference Texts Q3.
What are the advantages and the disadvantages of countries forming alliances to sell commodities such as oil?   (5)

ADVICE

(a) **Do not be put off** if you have not studied OPEC. From your knowledge of alliances and the information provided you should be able to answer the question fully.

(b) **Consider the effects from all angles** – the effects on the countries selling at a higher price, on the people living there; and the effects on the countries buying at a higher price, on the people and industries there; on developing countries, and so on.

Reference Table Q4

Exports of the Solomon Islands (percentage)		
Fish	35	Overseas price low
Timber	24	Will last only ten years
Copra	23	Falling world price
Palm oil	12	Badly affected by cyclones
Others	6	

Reference Texts Q4

Most of the Solomon Islands are covered with dense rainforest with coconut palms along the coast. There are 150 species of birds and 70 species of reptiles, while the seas are populated with colourful reef fish and many varieties of coral.

Most Solomon Islanders are subsistent, providing their own food crops, fish, meat, houses, fuel and canoes.

There are no real resort hotels and there is no way of handling a Boeing 747 full of tourists. If the Islanders are to develop tourism, it has to be done with great care so as not to damage their environment or culture.

Reference Map Q4: The location of the Solomon Islands

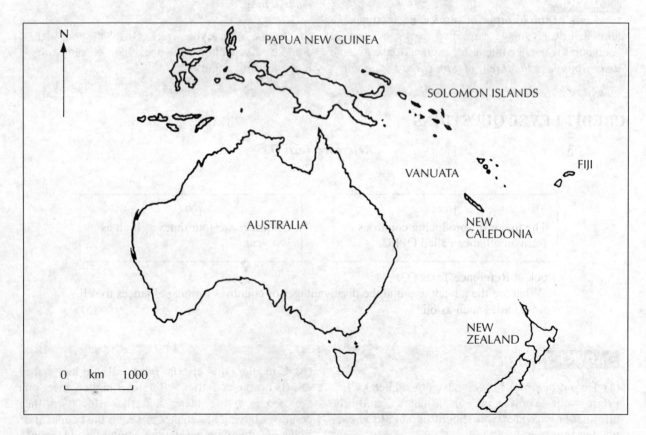

Reference Diagram Q4: The climate of the Solomon Islands

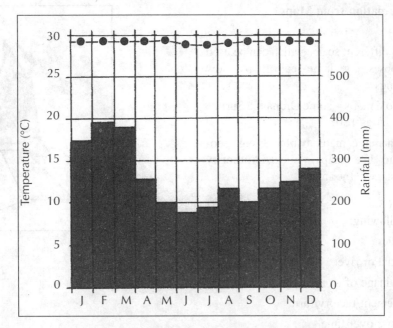

Look at Reference Table Q4, Texts Q4, Map Q4 and Diagram Q4.
Explain the arguments for and against the development of tourism in the Solomon Islands. (6)

ADVICE

(a) **Take your time.** Read all the information because it is all useful, e.g. the list of exports shows that the country is getting less and less money and therefore needs to develop other industries. The map shows you whether many tourists are likely to visit the Solomon Islands.

(b) **Organise your answer.** Begin with all the arguments for the development and state who would be in favour and then all the arguments against it. It may help you to jot down rough notes before you start your answer.

(c) **Expand the points you make.** Do not just repeat word for word the information in the resources, e.g. *'It will damage the culture and environment'*. Give details as well, e.g. *'More tourists will lead to more pollution which may damage the coral reefs'*.

▶ 4 IDENTIFYING GATHERING TECHNIQUES

These questions are concerned with choosing suitable methods of gathering (or researching) information on any topic within the Standard Grade course.

QUESTION PHRASING

The questions are often phrased as follows:

Give two techniques which you would use to gather relevant information on changes in land use/the relationship between land use and relief/the functions of a village. Justify your choice of techniques.

You are carrying out a study of two industrial areas/shopping centres/farms. Give two techniques you would use to gather information on how the industries/shops/farms in these two areas differ. Give a reason for each choice.

POINTS TO BEAR IN MIND

1 There are only a few gathering techniques which you need to know (see next page). You must memorize these so that you can choose the most appropriate ones for the question you are asked.

2 You must be able to justify your technique by giving more than a banal answer, such as *'because it would give you all the information you need'*. The advantages of each technique, given below, provide the basis for a more meaningful answer.

GATHERING TECHNIQUES YOU SHOULD KNOW

1 Extracting Information from Maps

INFORMATION

- there are maps of different scales which can be used for various purposes, e.g. large-scale maps show individual buildings
- you can also use old maps – some Ordnance Survey maps go back as far as 1801
- there are other thematic maps available, e.g. geology maps, land use maps, Local Authority development plans, weather maps

APPROPRIATE TOPICS
investigating the following:

- river characteristics
- landforms – glacial or river
- the relief and drainage of an area
- the site of a settlement/factory/farm
- changes in land use over time
- weather characteristics over Britain

ADVANTAGES

- maps are drawn at many scales and use many symbols, so they show a wealth of detail
- maps are drawn to scale and so are very accurate
- old maps provide reliable evidence of past land uses, so that changes can be investigated

2 Fieldsketching

INFORMATION

- when drawing a fieldsketch do not try and draw everything you see – concentrate on those features relevant to your study
- you do not need to be an artist to draw a sketch – use symbols or words if you cannot draw something realistically

APPROPRIATE TOPICS
investigating the following:

- the site and location of an industrial estate/shopping centre
- landforms in a small area, e.g. glacial or river features
- land uses on a farm/in a city centre
- building characteristics and quality

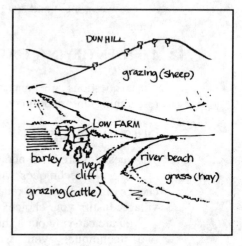

ADVANTAGES

- a fieldsketch is better than a photograph or map in that it can emphasise those aspects of the landscape you wish to highlight
- you can also omit from a fieldsketch unnecessary detail so that you can show the important points more clearly
- you can also include details which cannot be seen, e.g. air and noise pollution

3 Measuring Rivers

INFORMATION

- features of a river which can be simply measured are its width, depth, speed and size of bedload
- when measuring river features always choose a safe, shallow area and wear suitable clothes
- it is more accurate to take an average of several measurements than to take just one measurement

APPROPRIATE TOPICS

investigating the following:

- changes along a river
- the relationship between a river's characteristics, e.g. speed and bedload size, speed and width

ADVANTAGES

- it is the only way in which detailed statistics about most rivers can be gathered
- by taking an average of several measurements accurate readings can be obtained, allowing comparisons with other sites along the river

4 Measuring the Weather

INFORMATION

- it is possible to measure temperature (thermometer), precipitation (rain gauge), windspeed (anemometer), air pressure (barometer), sunshine (sunshine recorder) and humidity (hygrometer)
- measurements need to be taken at the same time daily to allow accurate comparison

APPROPRIATE TOPICS

investigating the following:

- changes in the weather over a period of time
- differences in the weather over a small area (a microclimate study) or in different parts of the country
- the relationship between elements of the weather, e.g. windspeed and air pressure, temperature and sunshine
- comparing actual weather with weather forecasts
- how the weather changes as a depression passes over

ADVANTAGES

- if the instruments are positioned in suitable locations, measurement provides an accurate record of the weather at a particular time
- many elements of the weather can be measured

5 Surveying Traffic

INFORMATION

- the amount of traffic along any street will vary (a) at different points along the street, (b) at different times of the day, and (c) on different days of the week
- when comparing the traffic on two streets, the survey should be undertaken at the same time and on the same day in both streets
- the traffic should be counted for at least ten minutes to obtain a reliable result
- a separate tally should be kept of different types of vehicle, e.g. cars, bikes, lorries, buses

investigating the following:

- differences in the volume of traffic along two or more streets
- comparing different land use zones of a town, e.g. a housing area and an industrial area
- the effects of a change in road management policy, e.g. a new bypass/one-way street system
- whether a settlement is a dormitory village

ADVANTAGES

- you can obtain first-hand, accurate and up-to-date information
- you can use the results to deduce the function of a settlement or area of a town from the amount of traffic, the type of traffic and how it varies during the day

6 Surveying Environmental Quality

INFORMATION

- many aspects of environmental quality can be observed in a survey, e.g. litter, noise, air pollution, graffiti, the amount of greenery, the state of the buildings
- it is possible to make up an index of environmental quality by giving marks out of ten for different aspects of the environment

APPROPRIATE TOPICS

investigating the following:

- differences in environmental quality between two or more areas
- comparing different land use zones of a town, e.g. inner city and suburbs

ADVANTAGES

- a survey provides you with first-hand, accurate, up-to-date information
- by making an index of environmental quality it is possible to compare two or more areas
- there are very few other ways of gathering information on some aspects of environmental quality, e.g. graffiti, litter

7 Surveying Buildings

INFORMATION

- you can survey many aspects of buildings, such as their use, number of storeys, wall materials, roof materials, number of chimneys, garages, gardens, signs of pollution
- take a large-scale map or draw a plan of each street beforehand so that you can record the characteristics of each building which is important in your survey

APPROPRIATE TOPICS

investigating the following:

- the age of buildings
- the functions of buildings
- the characteristics of different areas of town
- types of services found in settlement
- the distribution pattern of shops/services/industries within a town

ADVANTAGES

- by surveying the buildings, you obtain first-hand, accurate and up-to-date information
- you can deduce building age from building characteristics
- you can work out land use zones from a building survey

8 Compiling and Using a Questionnaire

INFORMATION

- to be able to draw valid conclusions from the questionnaire, you must ask a lot of people
- you can either stand in the street or go from house to house and ask questions
- do not ask a lot of questions
- ask precise questions which only need short answers
- ask a cross-section of people – young, middle-aged and old, male and female

APPROPRIATE TOPICS

investigating the following:

- people's shopping habits
- local people's views on a new development, e.g. a quarry, a shopping centre, a by-pass
- the main occupations in an area of town or in a village
- the population characteristics of an area – age, sex, place of work, how long people have lived there

ADVANTAGES

- by asking people questions you can find out (a) the most commonly held views, and (b) the range of views that people have
- by asking a sample of different people you can work out from their answers information about the whole population

9 Interviewing

INFORMATION

- interviews should be arranged in advance
- you should prepare and write down the questions beforehand
- the questions should allow you to find out detailed information

APPROPRIATE TOPICS

investigating the following:

- the characteristics of a farm/forest/recreation area
- the reasons behind the location of a factory/industrial estate/shopping centre
- arguments for and against a local controversial issue
- changes in an area over time, e.g. number of services in a village, types and methods of farming, housing characteristics

ADVANTAGES

- by asking one person many questions, you can find out detailed and reliable information
- by interviewing older people you can find out what an area used to be like and when and why it changed

GENERAL LEVEL QUESTIONS

<u>1</u> You are carrying out a study of two suburban shopping centres. As part of your study you have decided to:
  (i) compare the types of shop in the two shopping centres, and
  (ii) find out how people travel to the centres.
For each of these, give a technique you would use to gather information. Give a reason for each of your choices. (4)

ADVICE

(a) **Show off your knowledge.** Even though it does not tell you to give a different technique for each study you should do so, just to show the marker that you know two techniques. And, when you give a reason for your choice, tell the marker how this technique would provide the information you need, e.g. *a suitable technique for comparing the types of shop is to undertake a survey of each shopping centre because, by surveying each shop and recording its location on a plan of the centre, you can work out the number of shops of each type and their distribution. This information is also up-to-date.*

(b) **Make the most appropriate choice.** Always choose the technique that gives you the most to write about. For example, to study how people travel to a shopping centre, suitable techniques include: 1. extracting information from maps (to find the transport available), 2. a questionnaire of shoppers, 3. interviewing the shopping centre managers, 4. a survey of transport facilities (noting down car parks, taxi ranks, bus stops, etc.). From these, choose the one that you can justify in the most detail and so earn the most marks.

CREDIT LEVEL QUESTIONS

<u>2</u> Give two techniques you would use to gather information on changes in land use in an inner-city area during the last thirty years.
Give reasons for your choice of techniques. (4)

ADVICE

(a) **Make your points clearly.** One mark is available for each technique so, although it says 'give a technique', make sure that you describe the technique clearly enough to earn that one mark. For example, *'Two techniques are looking at maps and interviewing people'* is too vague to deserve marks. It would be better, instead, to write: *'Two suitable techniques would be to compare old and new maps of*

the area and also to interview people who have lived or worked in the area for thirty years'.

(b) **Play safe.** The question does not make it clear whether you have to give reasons (plural) for each technique or just one reason for each technique. So, when in doubt, play safe and make the extra point.

<u>3</u> Which techniques would you use to investigate whether a village is a retirement centre? Justify your choices. (4)

ADVICE

Do not be put off if you have not studied this before. Mentally, go through the techniques you have memorised and work out which ones would provide you with some relevant information. For example, a questionnaire to find out people's ages and

occupations, a building survey to find out the number of old people's homes, retirement homes, places of work, an interview with an employee in the Council's social services department.

These questions are concerned with choosing suitable methods of processing information relating to any topic within the Standard Grade syllabus.

QUESTION PHRASING

The questions are often phrased as follows:

Changes in population structure in a Scottish city			
	age-groups		
year	*0–14*	*15–59*	*60+*
1950	31	62	7
1960	29	62	9
1970	26	65	9
1980	24	65	11
1990	23	64	13

Identify a relevant technique to illustrate the information above. Justify your choice.

Land uses in a typical CBD	
offices	40%
comparison shops	30%
convenience shops	15%
public buildings	10%
industry	5%

Give one type of graph you would use to show the information above. Give a reason for your choice.

What techniques would you use to show the relationship between land use and relief/changes in land use/changes in temperature? Give reasons for your answer.

POINTS TO BEAR IN MIND

1 Just as for gathering techniques, there are only a few processing techniques which you need to know (see next page). You must memorise these as well and then you will be able to select the most suitable technique for the question asked.

2 You will also have to justify your choice of technique and, again, you must avoid making simplistic statements such as: because it is easy to draw; because it looks good, or because that is how this information is always shown. Look at the advantages of each technique, given below, for clues to better answers.

PROCESSING TECHNIQUES YOU SHOULD KNOW

1 Bar Graphs

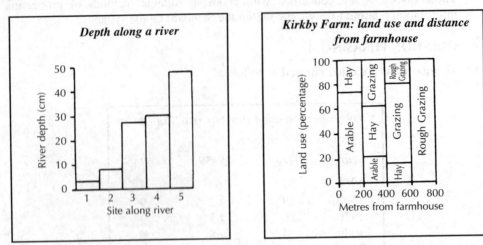

Depth along a river

Kirkby Farm: land use and distance from farmhouse

INFORMATION
● a bar graph is used to compare the amounts of several different items
● a divided bar graph is used to show how one amount is divided up

APPROPRIATE TOPICS (BAR GRAPHS)
investigating the following:
● sunshine over several days/months
● rainfall over several days/months
● width/depth at different points along a river
● the number of people with different views about a local issue

APPROPRIATE TOPICS (DIVIDED BAR GRAPHS)
investigating the following:
● the number/% of people in different occupations
● the number/% of people using different forms of transport
● the amounts/% of different exports from a country
● the number/% of people in different age-groups

ADVANTAGES
● by showing amounts side by side, it is easy to compare their importance
● shading each column or bar makes the graph even clearer
● accurate statistics can be read off the graph

2 Population Pyramids
INFORMATION
● a population pyramid is used to show the number or percentage of males and females in each age-group in a region or country
● it is a type of bar graph, with horizontal bars drawn for males and females
● the age-groups are usually five years

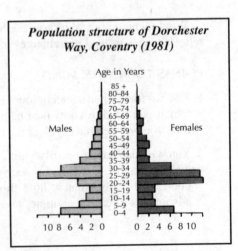

Population structure of Dorchester Way, Coventry (1981)

APPROPRIATE TOPICS
investigating the following:
● the population structure of a region or country
● birth-rates and death-rates in a country
● a comparison of the standards of living in two regions or countries

ADVANTAGES
● it clearly shows the number of males and females in each age-group and makes it possible to quickly compare the population structures of two areas
● shading of the bars makes the information even clearer
● it is possible to deduce many population characteristics from the shape of the pyramid (e.g. birth-rates, death-rates, migration movements)
● accurate statistics can be read off the pyramid

3 Line Graphs

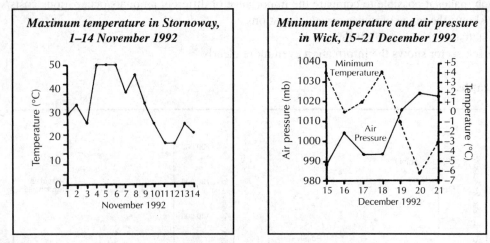

Maximum temperature in Stornoway, 1–14 November 1992

Minimum temperature and air pressure in Wick, 15–21 December 1992

INFORMATION
- a line graph is used to show changes in an amount over distance or time
- a multiple line graph shows several lines on the same graph

APPROPRIATE TOPICS (LINE GRAPHS)
investigating the following:
- changes in the number of workers/farms/services/imports over time
- changes in the value of land with distance from the city centre
- changes in river speed with distance from the source

APPROPRIATE TOPICS (MULTIPLE LINE GRAPHS)
investigating the following:
- changes in temperature and air pressure over several days
- changes in farm workers and farm machinery over many years
- changes in the volume of imports and exports over several years

ADVANTAGES
- line graphs clearly show changes and trends
- accurate statistics can be read off a line graph
- by showing several graphs together as a multiple line graph, any relationships between two or more changing amounts can be identified

4 Pie-Graphs

INFORMATION
- a pie-graph shows how one amount is divided up and it is used in the same way as a divided bar graph
- the larger the slice or segment, the bigger the amount
- each amount has to be worked out in degrees, and the total must add up to 360

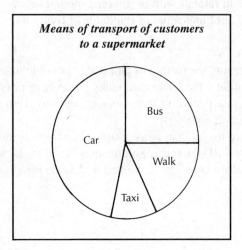

Means of transport of customers to a supermarket

APPROPRIATE TOPICS
investigating the following:
- a farmer's different costs in a year
- methods of transport used by workers/shoppers
- bedload of different sizes in a river
- the proportion of people in different types of occupations/sectors of industry
- people's different views on a local issue

ADVANTAGES

● a pie-graph makes it possible to compare the importance of different amounts/occupations/costs/views
● it clearly shows the range of views/costs/occupations
● accurate statistics can be read off the graph
● shading each sector shows the information even more clearly

5 Scattergraphs

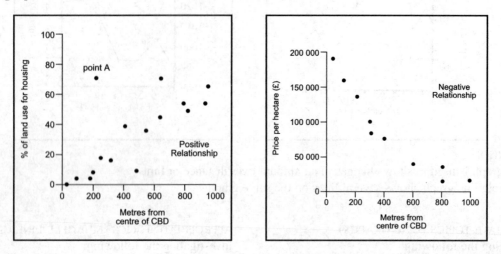

INFORMATION

● on a scattergraph points are plotted in the same way as for a line graph, but the points are not joined up
● a scattergraph is used to show if there is a connection or relationship between one set of numbers and another
● from the points plotted it is possible to see whether there is a pattern – a pattern exists if one set of numbers generally increases with the other set or if one set of numbers generally decreases with the other set (see scattergraphs above)

APPROPRIATE TOPICS

investigating the following:
● the price of land and distance from the city centre
● the number of vehicles and distance from the city centre
● building height and distance from the city centre
● changes in rainfall with height on a mountainside
● two different indicators of standards of living for several countries

ADVANTAGES

● by observing the pattern of points it is possible to see whether there is a relationship between the two sets of information – the relationship may be positive or negative
● if there is a pattern to the points, exceptions from that pattern can also be easily identified (e.g. point A in scattergraph 1 above)
● it is more useful than a line graph when there is more than one value for each amount, e.g. at one kilometre from the CBD the traffic volume may be 500 vehicles per hour on one road and 800 per hour on another road – this information can be plotted on a scattergraph but not on a single line graph

6 Land Use Maps

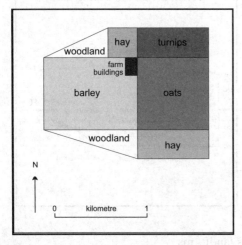

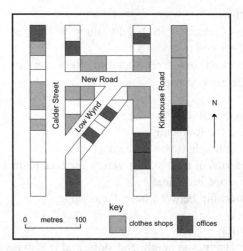

INFORMATION
- a land use map may show all the land uses in an area or just selected ones
- it can be used in towns as well as the countryside

APPROPRIATE TOPICS
investigating the following:
- the distribution pattern of shops/terraced housing/forestry/recreation facilities/factories/arable land
- the importance of different land uses in an area
- the relationship between land use and distance from the CBD/steepness/height

ADVANTAGES
- it clearly shows the importance of different land uses in an area
- by only including the land uses you are studying, their distribution pattern is much clearer
- it shows the distribution pattern of land uses
- it will show any relationship between the land uses, e.g. which types of shop are found near one another
- it shows the land uses which cluster together and those which are more dispersed

7 Dot Distribution Maps

INFORMATION
- a dot distribution map shows the locations of a feature over an area
- each dot can represent a single, exact location (e.g. dairy farms) or represent the approximate location of many (e.g. a dot can represent where every 1000 people live)
- different coloured dots can show different features
- dot distribution maps may be of very wide areas or of just a few streets

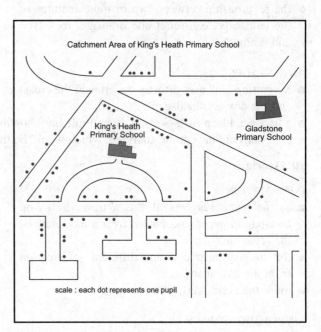

APPROPRIATE TOPICS
investigating the following:
- the distribution of physical features, e.g. drumlins, erratics
- the distribution of human features, e.g market gardens, 19th century housing, population, combine harvesters

ADVANTAGES
- it clearly shows the distribution of a feature over an area
- by using different coloured dots, several distribution patterns can be shown and any relationship between them identified, e.g. distribution of coal mines and steelworks
- the map could also include contour lines/soil type/rainfall so that any relationship between the distribution pattern and the physical landscape can be easily spotted

8 Cross-Sections

INFORMATION
- this shows changes in height along a line of section between two points
- it is worked out from contour lines on an Ordnance Survey map

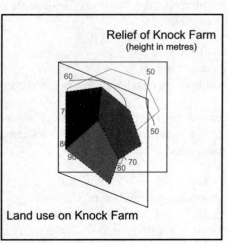

Section across the Devon Valley

Height (in metres)

300 — Bank Hill
200 — Village River Dollarbeg
of Dollar → Devon Farm
100 —
0 —

Horizontal Scale: 1 cm = 0·6km

APPROPRIATE TOPICS
investigating the following:
- changes in height across an area
- the landforms of an area, e.g. valley, plateau, plain
- types of slope in an area
- the relationship between height and slope

ADVANTAGES
- it shows changes in height and slope and it also reveals landforms
- the section can be annotated (labelled) to highlight those aspects of the relief being studied
- other features can also be labelled on the section to show any relationship between them and the relief
- a section is used to show the typical relief of an area without having to analyse the whole area (it is a sample)

9 Transects

INFORMATION
- a transect is a line along which features of the human and/or physical landscape are located
- as a processing technique, a transect consists of a cross-section with additional information written above it or, more usually, in rows below it

Transect Across the Devon Valley

Bank Hill

300 —
200 —
100 — flood plain River
Devon
0 —

SETTLEMENT			village of Dollar			farm
COMMUNICATIONS	footpaths only	A91 and streets		farm tracks	secondary and minor roads	
OTHER LAND USES	rough grazing	golf course		farm land	forestry	

APPROPRIATE TOPICS
investigating the following:
- changes in land use across an area
- the relationship between the physical landscape and land uses
- the relationship between two or more features of the landscape, e.g. relief and drainage, rock type and drainage

ADVANTAGES
- by putting land uses directly underneath the cross-section, it is easy to see the relationship between land uses and the physical landscape
- a transect, like a cross-section, is a sample line showing typical changes across an area and it means the whole area does not have to be analysed, which would be much more complex

10 Overlays

INFORMATION
- as the name suggests, this is a map, drawn on transparent paper, and placed over a base map of the same area
- the overlay map contains different information from the base map
- more than one overlay can be used

Relief of Knock Farm
(height in metres)

60
50
7
50
8
90 70
80

Land use on Knock Farm

APPROPRIATE TOPICS
investigating the following:
- the growth of a settlement
- changes in the location of an industry over time
- the relationship between land use and the physical landscape in an area

ADVANTAGES

- by having different aspects of an area on different maps, they can be viewed separately or together
- the overlays will make it easy to identify any relationship between the features on the different maps, e.g. relief on a base map and land uses on the overlay
- the overlays can represent different time-periods and show the growth of a geographical feature (e.g. a settlement) or changes in location (e.g. of an iron and steel industry, port activity, coal mines)

GENERAL LEVEL QUESTIONS

Reference Table Q1

Land uses on Foinavon Farm (%)			
barley	20	woodland	10
oats	25	grassland	30
turnips	15		

1 As part of a farm study, you have collected the information shown in Reference Table Q1 above.

Give one type of graph you would use to show this information and give a reason for your choice. (3)

ADVICE

(a) **Read the key words carefully.** The question does not ask you to *draw* a graph, just to *give* a type of graph. If you have memorised all the types of graph given above, you should be able to name a pie-graph or a divided bar graph as the most suitable ones for this information.

(b) **Check the number of marks.** You can only earn one mark by naming a suitable graph, so two marks must be awarded for giving a single reason. Make sure, therefore, that you give a full, developed reason worthy of two marks. For example, '*A pie-graph is ideal for showing how one amount is divided up. It clearly shows all the land uses and makes it possible to compare their importance. Shading in the segments makes the graph even clearer. Percentage figures can also be worked out from the angle of each segment.*'

2 By using a questionnaire you have found out where the customers live who use a shopping centre in the suburbs of your local town. What processing technique would best show where the customers live? Give a reason for your answer. (3)

ADVICE

Give detailed answers. The most obvious answer is a map of some kind, but do not just write '*map*'. You should give the type of map, such as a distribution map, an isopleth map or a ray diagram. And, for your reason, describe how your chosen processing technique would show the information. For example, '*A suitable processing technique is a dot distribution map. With this type of map the address of each customer can be shown precisely by a dot so that the distribution pattern can be clearly seen. This can then be emphasised by drawing a line around all of the dots to show the extent of the sphere of influence. The map shows not only how large is the sphere of influence but from which directions most and fewest customers come.*'

CREDIT LEVEL QUESTIONS

<u>3</u> What techniques would you use to show the relationship between land use and relief on a farm?
Justify your choices. (4)

Reference Table Q4: Changes in
Employment Structure in a Scottish Town

year	primary %	secondary %	tertiary %
1950	12	50	38
1960	11	45	44
1970	8	36	56
1980	4	32	64
1990	2	28	70

<u>4</u> Identify two techniques to illustrate the information in Reference Table Q4. Give reasons for your choices. (4)

MAPWORK QUESTIONS

Every Standard Grade examination paper contains mapwork questions. They are usually, but not always, the first questions in the paper and they make up approximately one fifth of the total marks. A variety of maps are used in the examination. The most common are Ordnance Survey maps, usually of scale 1:50,000 or of scale 1:25,000, but other maps such as road maps, street maps and tourist maps are used occasionally. Mapwork questions fit into the seven types of question already covered, but they do require particular skills and therefore deserve separate attention.

QUESTION PHRASING

The mapwork questions are often phrased as follows:

Match the glacial features with their correct grid references.

Using map evidence, explain the growth of settlement X.

Complete the cross-section by marking the exact location of the following features: ....

Describe the distribution of settlement on the map.

Which type of farming is likely to be practised at farm Y?

What are the advantages and the disadvantages of locating a saw-mill at place Z?

POINTS TO BEAR IN MIND

1 You need to be able to work out 4-figure and 6-figure grid references and to be able to interpret contour lines. You also need to be able to recognise landforms and land use zones in towns.

2 Although a key is provided with the map, it is helpful to know the most common symbols on Ordnance Survey maps – so that you will save time in the examination.

3 Do not be put off by a map of a different type from those which you have used in class. The questions test your map skills and you should be able to work out all the answers by looking at the map and its key.

4 Remember to give grid references when referring to locations on the map.

GENERAL LEVEL QUESTIONS

For all these questions look at the Ordance Survey map of Kilbirnie on page 40.

1 Look at the buildings in squares 3155 and 3253.
> One of the squares shows a new housing area. The other shows an old industrial area.
> (a) (i) Which square shows new housing?
>   (ii) Which square shows old industry?
> (b) Explain your choices for both squares. (KU, 4)

ADVICE

(a) **Use map evidence**. The map shows the shapes of buildings, the street pattern, and the nearness to railway lines and to services. Use this evidence to make your choices.

(b) **Give a full answer**. When you have explained why you think the new housing is in square 3155, do not say 'Therefore the other square must contain old industry'. To get full marks, you must give reasons for both your choices.

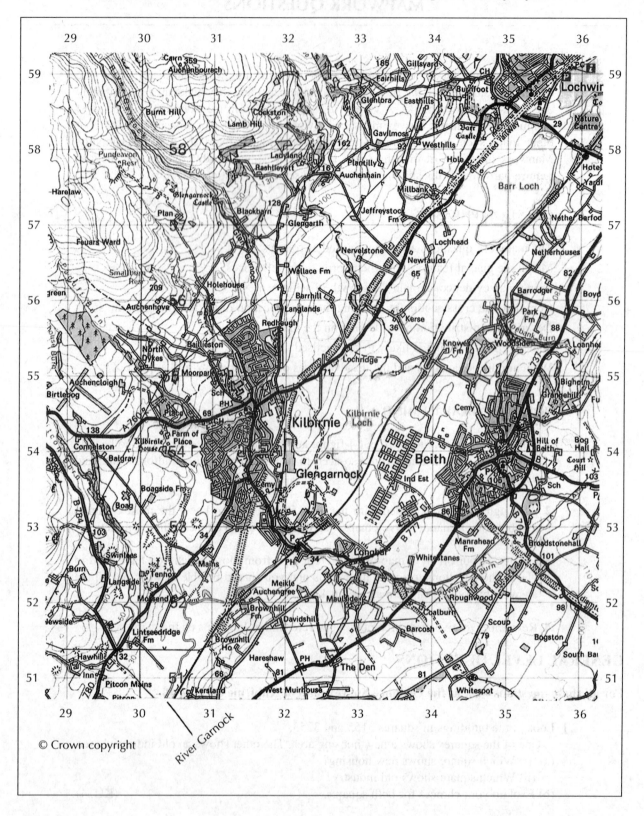

© Crown copyright

2 What are the advantages and disadvantages of square 3353 as a location for an industrial estate? (ES, 4)

> **ADVICE**
>
> (a) **Use map evidence.** The map shows you the suitability of the land for building, the nearness to communications, and the nearness to a housing area. Use this evidence in your answer.
>
> (b) **Expand your answer.** Instead of saying *'One advantage is that the land is gently sloping'*, go on to say *'This makes it easy to build on, and provides suitable land for expansion.'*

CREDIT LEVEL QUESTIONS

1 Describe the changes in the physical characteristics of the Garnock Burn and its valley between GR 295590 and GR 305510. (ES, 6)

> **ADVICE**
>
> (a) **Use map evidence.** The map shows the river width, straightness, tributaries and landforms, such as an ox-bow lake. This is evidence of the physical characteristics of the river. It also shows the steepness and height of the valley sides and the width of the valley floor. This is evidence of the characteristics of its valley.
>
> (b) **Look out for the key words** – for *'changes'* do not just describe the river's characteristics, but say
>
> how they change from north to south. For *'physical characteristics'* write about the natural features, and not about land uses such as farming, forestry and settlement.
>
> (c) **Organise your answer.** You may find it easier to write firstly about the changes in the physical characteristics and then about the changes in the river valley.

2 Compare the probable types of farming at Knowes (GR 342553) and Plan (GR 305571). (ES, 6)

> **ADVICE**
>
> (a) **Use map evidence.** From the map you can work out the slope, the height (and so the temperature and rainfall), the communications, and the drainage. Use this evidence to explain the likely types of farming at the two locations.
>
> (b) **Give reasons.** Even though the question asks
>
> you to *'compare'*; you must still give your reasons for choosing two different types of farming.
>
> (c) **Show off your knowledge.** Instead of just saying *'Farming at Plan is probably hill-sheep because the land is steep'*, go on to say *'This makes it difficult to use machinery and so makes arable farming impossible.'*

SUMMARY

In this chapter you have been given a lot of advice on how to tackle different types of examination questions. If you cannot remember all this advice when going into the examination, at least remember this:

Always assume that the marker knows nothing!

If you think that the person who will read your answer is totally ignorant, then you will surely remember to explain all your answers in the greatest detail and with the utmost clarity.

CHAPTER THREE

THE SYLLABUS

INTRODUCTION

▶ THE GEOGRAPHY STANDARD GRADE SYLLABUS

The Geography Standard Grade syllabus is divided into three sections – *The Physical Environment, The Human Environment* and *International Issues*. Each section is broken down into several broad ideas, called Key Ideas. There are 17 Key Ideas altogether and they make up the syllabus which you learn during your coursework in school. Each Key Idea itself can be broken down into smaller ideas which you must understand (**Understanding**) and which require knowledge of much factual information (**Knowledge**). The questions in the examinations test your Knowledge and Understanding of these Key Ideas, and they also test your ability to use these ideas and facts to solve geographical problems (**Enquiry Skills**).

A   THE PHYSICAL ENVIRONMENT

Key Idea 1   Physical landscapes
Key Idea 2   Weather
Key Idea 3   Climates
Key Idea 4   The physical environment and human activities
Key Idea 5   Land use conflicts
Key Idea 6   Global environmental issues

B   THE HUMAN ENVIRONMENT

Key Idea 7   Settlement characteristics
Key Idea 8   Urban change
Key Idea 9   Farming
Key Idea 10   Manufacturing industry
Key Idea 11   Economic change

C   INTERNATIONAL ISSUES

Key Idea 12   Population distribution
Key Idea 13   Population characteristics
Key Idea 14   Population change
Key Idea 15   International relations
Key Idea 16   International trade
Key Idea 17   International aid and self-help

In order to help you with your revision, this chapter describes the main aspects of each Key Idea, includes some of the vocabulary you must know, and provides examples of typical examination questions which relate to each Key Idea.

A   THE PHYSICAL ENVIRONMENT

▶ KEY IDEA 1   THE PHYSICAL LANDSCAPES OF RIVERS AND GLACIATED AREAS

WHAT YOU NEED TO KNOW AND UNDERSTAND

You need to know about the following:

1 Features of glacial erosion.
2 Features of glacial deposition.
3 Features of river erosion.
4 Features of river deposition.
5 Processes by which ice erodes and deposits.
6 Processes by which rivers erode and deposit.

VOCABULARY

Abrasion   is the process by which rocks in rivers or moving ice scrape the rock surface over which they are moving and erode it.

Alluvial fan   is an accumulation of alluvium by a river when it flows from a steep slope on to a plain.

Alluvium   is material deposited by a river.

Arête   is a narrow mountain ridge between two corries.

Attrition   is the process by which rocks in a river or in the sea are worn by constantly rubbing against each other.

Boulder clay   is the moraine left behind by a glacier or ice-sheet when it melts.

Braiding   is the splitting of a river into different channels.

Corrasion   is the process by which rivers or waves use the rocks they carry to batter the land.

Corrie   is an armchair-shaped hollow at the head of a glaciated mountain valley.

Crag and tail   is a hill with one very steep side, which once faced an ice-sheet, and a long, gently-sloping side which was protected from glacial erosion.

Delta   is an area of alluvium formed at the mouth of a river.

Deposition   is the laying down of rocks by moving agents.

Distributary   is a branch of a river which flows out of the river.

Drumlin   is a smooth, oval hill made of glacial deposits, usually steeper on the upstream side.

Erosion   wearing away of rocks by moving agents.

Erratic   is a rock transported by ice and deposited on a rock surface of a different type.

Esker   is a long ridge of sand and gravel, laid down by a river which ran under an ice-sheet.

Estuary   is the tidal mouth of a river usually formed by a relative rise in sea-level.

Fiord   is a U-shaped valley drowned by the sea to become a deep, narrow sea-inlet.

Flood-plain   is a wide valley beside a river made up of alluvium deposited in times of flood.

Freeze-thaw action   is the weathering process by which the repeated freezing and thawing of water in cracks causes the rock to break up.

Frost action   is another name for freeze-thaw action.

Glacier   is a body of moving ice in an upland area.

Ground moraine   is the accumulation of rock particles between the bottom of a glacier and the underlying rock.

Hanging valley   is a tributary valley, the end of which is well above the main valley which was deepened by a glacier.

Ice-sheet   is a large body of moving ice in a lowland area.

Interlocking spurs   are pieces of rock which jut into a valley from alternate directions so that, when looking upstream, they appear to interlock.

Landform   is a feature made by natural processes.

Lateral moraine   is the accumulation of rock particles on the surface of a glacier at its sides.

Long profile   of a river is a section of the course of a river showing its slope from source to mouth.

Mass movement   is the movement of rocks and soil by gravity.

Meander   is a loop-like bend in the course of a river.

Medial moraine   is the accumulation of rock particles on the surface of a glacier in the middle.

Moraine-dammed lake   is a lake ponded back behind a hill of moraine.

Mouth   of a river is the point where it ends.

Natural levee   is an embankment beside a river built up by deposition of alluvium.

Outwash plain   is a plain composed of material washed out of a melting glacier or ice-sheet.

Outwash sands   is another name for outwash plain.

Ox-bow lake   is a former meander of a river.

Physical landscape   is the natural scenery of an area.

Plucking   is the process by which moving ice tears away rocks on to which it has frozen.

Pyramidal peak   is the pointed summit of a mountain, formed by three corries back to back.

Rejuvenation   is the increase in erosive activity of a river due to a relative fall in sea-level.

Ria   is a V-shaped valley drowned by the sea to become a deep sea-inlet.

River beach   is the accumulation of material deposited by a river along its course.

River cliff   is the steep bank of a river formed through erosion.

River terrace   is a flat bench lying above and on each side of a river valley.

Roche moutonnée   is a large rock smoothed by ice on its upstream side, jagged on its downstream side.

Scree   is the accumulation of loose material at the bottom of a steep slope.

Snow-line   is the line above which snow remains permanently.

Source   of the river is the point where it begins.

Till   is another name for boulder clay.

Transportation   is the carrying of rock particles.

Tributary   is a smaller river which flows into a larger one.

Truncated spur   is a piece of rock which once jutted into a valley but is eroded away by a glacier.

U-shaped valley   is a valley with steep sides and a flat base, once occupied by a glacier.

V-shaped valley   is a valley which is V-shaped in cross-section, typical of a river in its youthful stage.

Waterfall   is a steep and marked fall along the course of a river.

Weathering   is the process by which rocks are worn away but not transported away.

GENERAL LEVEL QUESTIONS

1   *Reference Diagram Q1: Features of upland glaciation*

(a) Look at Reference Diagram Q1.

It shows four features of glacial erosion, labelled A to D. Complete the following table by matching the letters with their correct descriptions.   (KU, 3)

Feature of glacial erosion	Letter
Hanging valley Corrie Truncated spur Arête	

(b) For any one of the features named in the table above, explain how it has formed. You may use a diagram or diagrams to illustrate your answer.   (KU, 4)

Reproduced with kind permission of Aerofilms Ltd.

Look at the photograph.
(a) Is the river in its upper course or in its lower course?
(b) Give two reasons for your answer.   (KU, 2)

CREDIT LEVEL QUESTIONS

<u>3</u>   *Reference Diagram Q3: A glaciated lowland landscape*

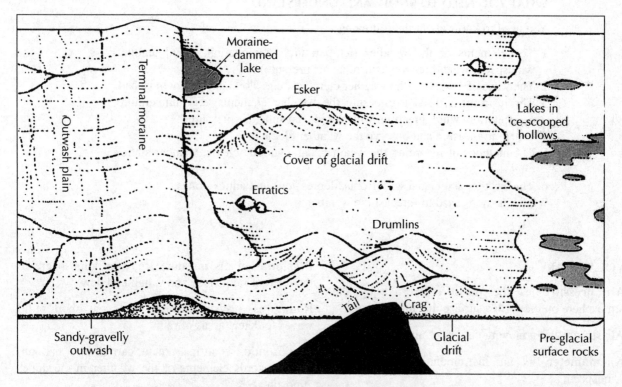

Look at Reference Diagram Q3 above. It shows a glaciated lowland landscape.
(a) In which direction was the ice moving?
(b) Give detailed reasons for your answer.   (KU, 4)

<u>4</u>   *Reference Table Q4: Characteristics of the River Slitrig*

	Upper course	*Middle course*	*Lower course*
River width	2 metres	5 metres	7 metres
River load	Medium-sized; jagged	Large-sized; quite round	Small-sized; rounded
River depth	0.5 metres	1.5 metres	1.2 metres
Valley width	20 metres	15 metres	50 metres

Look at Reference Table Q4. It shows some of the characteristics of the River Slitrig in the Borders Region.
    Compare the changes along the course of the River Slitrig with those of a typical river.   (ES, 4)

► KEY IDEA 2   THE ELEMENTS OF THE WEATHER AND WEATHER PATTERNS

WHAT YOU NEED TO KNOW AND UNDERSTAND

You need to know about the following:

1 The elements of the weather (temperature, precipitation, cloud amount, windspeed, wind direction, sunshine, air pressure).
2 The ways of observing the weather elements, e.g. cloud amount, windspeed.
3 The instruments used to measure the weather elements, e.g. temperature, precipitation, wind direction, windspeed, sunshine, air pressure.
4 Where to measure and observe the weather elements.
5 The methods of recording the weather, e.g. synoptic charts, weather station circles.
6 The weather associated with fronts, depressions and anticyclones.
7 The methods used to forecast the weather.

VOCABULARY

Air pressure is the pressure exerted by the atmosphere on the earth's surface due to its weight.

Air stream is a moving current of air.

Anemometer is an instrument for measuring windspeed.

Anticyclone is an area of high atmospheric pressure.

Barometer/barograph is an instrument for measuring air pressure and, in the case of the barograph, for recording the air pressure.

Beaufort scale is a scale of wind force, from 0 to 12.

Celsius scale is another name for the Centigrade scale of temperature.

Cold front is a boundary where cold air is undercutting warm air in a depression.

Depression is a low pressure system.

Humidity is the amount of water vapour in the atmosphere.

Hygrometer is an instrument which measures relative humidity.

Isobar is a line joining places with equal air pressure.

Millibar is a unit of pressure used in recording air pressure.

Occluded front is where the cold front overtakes the warm front in a depression.

Okta is a fraction of the sky covered in cloud, expressed in eighths of the total sky covered.

Precipitation is moisture from the atmosphere in the form of rain, sleet, snow, hail and dew.

Radar is a system which sends out short radio waves to detect areas of rain.

Radiosonde is an instrument, carried by a balloon, which records elements of the weather in the upper atmosphere.

Rain gauge is an instrument for measuring rainfall.

Stevenson screen is a wooden box on legs, painted white, in which weather instruments are placed.

Sunshine recorder is an instrument for measuring the hours of sunshine.

Synoptic chart is a chart or map showing the weather conditions at a specific time.

Temperature is the degree of heat or cold in the atmosphere.

Thermometer is an instrument for measuring temperature.

Warm front is a boundary where warm air is rising over cold air in a depression.

Warm sector is a wedge of warm air in a depression.

Weather element is a constituent that makes up the weather, e.g. temperature, rainfall.

Weather satellite is recording equipment in orbit around the earth which sends back pictures of cloud cover.

Weather station is a site where different elements of the weather are measured and recorded.

Weather station circle is a series of symbols which show the weather at a specific location.

1   *Reference Map Q1: Weather conditions in the British Isles, 26 December 1992*

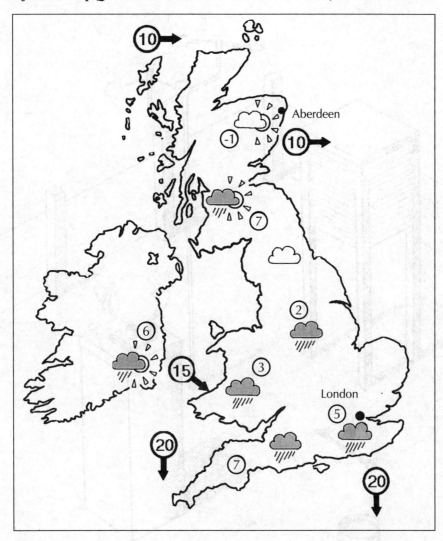

Reference Diagram Q1: Weather station circle for Aberdeen

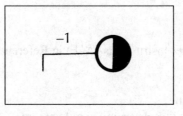

Look at Reference Map Q1 and Reference Diagram Q1.

Reference Diagram Q1 is a weather station circle for Aberdeen on 26 December 1992. Using Reference Map Q1, draw another weather station circle for London on the same day.   (KU, 4)

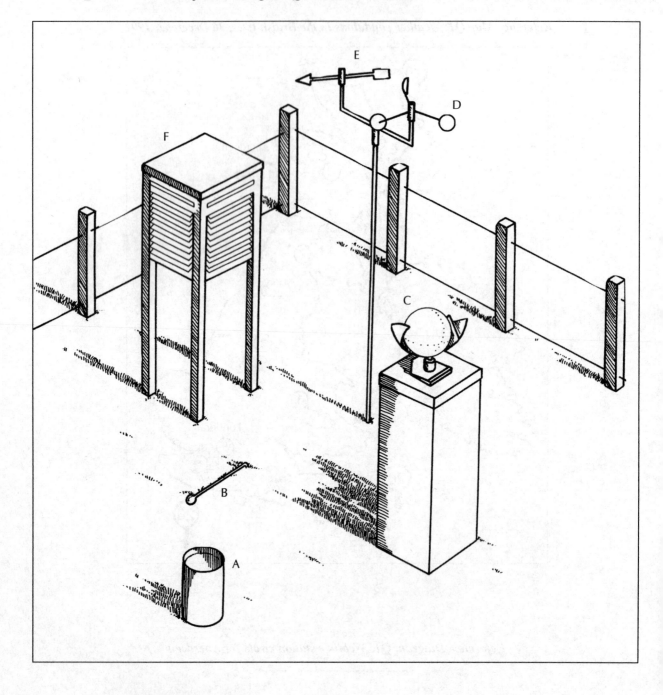

(a) Which of the weather instruments (A–F) in Reference Diagram Q2 measures:
   (i) precipitation?
   (ii) windspeed?
   (iii) hours of sunshine?   (KU, 3)
(b) Describe one method of observing cloud amount.   (KU, 2)

CREDIT LEVEL QUESTIONS

3   *Reference Diagram Q3: Possible locations for a weather station*

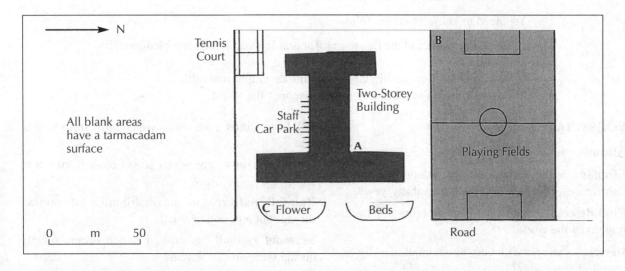

Look at Reference Diagram Q3. It shows three possible locations for a weather station, A, B and C.
(a) Which is the best location? (b) Give detailed reasons for your answer.   (ES, 4)

4   *Reference Diagram Q4: Synoptic chart for western Europe*

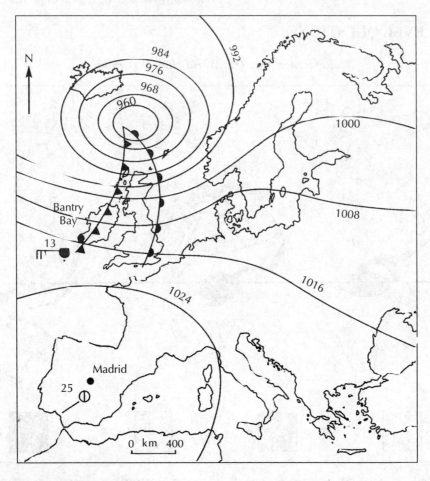

Look at Reference Diagram Q4.
    Explain the differences in weather conditions being experienced at Bantry Bay and Madrid.   (KU, 5)

▶ KEY IDEA 3   THE MAJOR CLIMATIC REGIONS OF THE WORLD

WHAT YOU NEED TO KNOW AND UNDERSTAND

You need to know about the following:

1 The characteristics of the Equatorial, Tundra, Tropical Desert and Mediterranean climates.
2 How to identify these climates from climate graphs and tables.
3 The distribution of these climates throughout the world.

VOCABULARY

Altitude   is the height above sea-level.

Climate   is the average weather conditions a place experiences, usually worked out over thirty years.

Cold desert   is a term used to describe the Tundra regions of the world.

Desert   is an area with very low rainfall, usually less than 250 mm a year.

Drought   is a long period of dry weather.

Extreme climate   is a climate with a large range of temperature between its hottest and coldest months.

Latitude   is the angular distance of a place from the Equator.

Offshore winds   are winds which blow from land to sea.

Onshore winds   are winds which blow from sea to land.

Rainfall pattern   is the distribution of rainfall throughout a period of time.

Seasonal rainfall   is rainfall which occurs mostly during one part of the year.

Temperature range   is the difference between the maximum and minimum temperature.

Tropics   is the area between the Tropic of Cancer ($23\frac{1}{2}°$N) and the Tropic of Capricorn ($23\frac{1}{2}°$S).

Tundra   is the area between the northern limit of tree growth and the region of permanent snow and ice.

GENERAL LEVEL QUESTIONS

<u>1</u>   *Reference Map Q1: World climate regions*

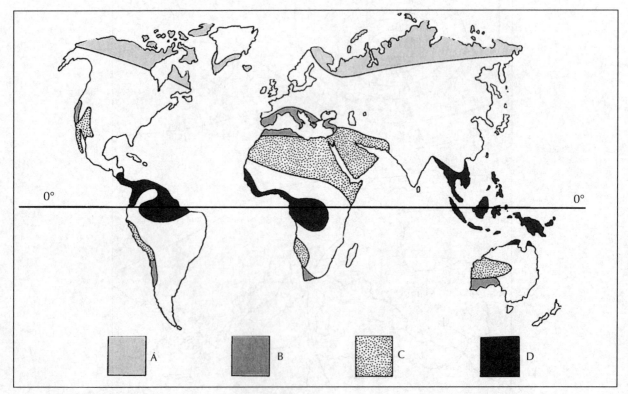

Reference Map Q1 shows four climatic regions, labelled from A to D.
Match the four climates below with their correct letter:
(a) Equatorial.   (b) Tundra.   (c) Tropical Desert.   (d) Mediterranean.   (KU, 3)

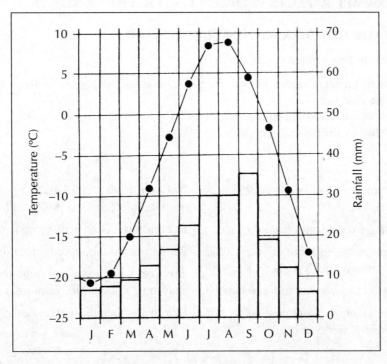

Describe the main features of the climate shown in Reference Diagram Q2.   (ES, 3)

CREDIT LEVEL QUESTIONS

3 Describe the similarities and differences between a Tropical Desert and a Mediterranean climate.
(KU, 4)

4   *Reference Diagram Q4: A climate graph for Nairobi (1° S)*

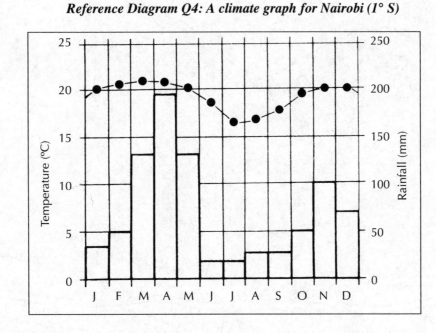

'Lying very close to the Equator, Nairobi displays the characteristics of a typical Equatorial climate.'

Look at Reference Diagram Q4 and the statement above.
    Do you agree with the statement above? Give reasons for your answer.   (ES, 4)

WHAT YOU NEED TO KNOW AND UNDERSTAND

You need to know about the following:

1 How the physical landscape (e.g. steepness of slope, height, soil) affects the way the land is used.
2 How climate affects people's activities.
3 How the weather affects people's activities.

VOCABULARY

Country park   is a small area of countryside near a city set aside for recreation.

Drainage   is removing excess water from the land.

Forestry Commission   is the organisation responsible for planting and maintaining forests in the U.K.

Irrigation   is putting extra water on to farmland.

Land use   is the way in which people use an area of land, e.g. farming, forestry, settlement.

National Park   is a large area of countryside whose outstanding scenery is protected for public enjoyment.

Recreation   is an activity undertaken for pleasure.

Rural   is the adjective to describe the countryside.

Terraces   are steps cut into the hillside to make additional flat land for farming.

Urban   is the adjective to describe towns.

GENERAL LEVEL QUESTIONS

4   *Reference Diagram Q1: Possible land uses in the Scottish Highlands*

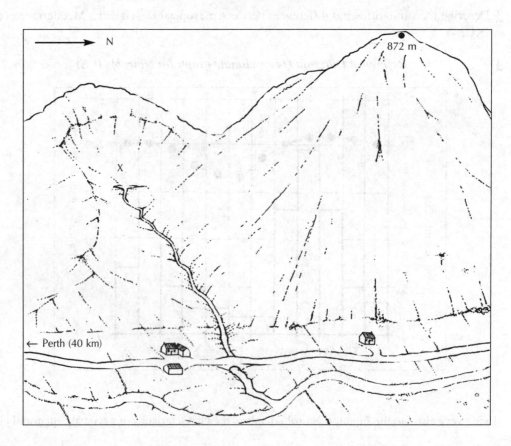

Look at Reference Diagram Q1.
      Which land use would be more suitable for area X – a reservoir or a forestry plantation? Give reasons for your answer.

(ES, 4)

Reference Map Q2: Weather conditions in the British Isles, December 1992

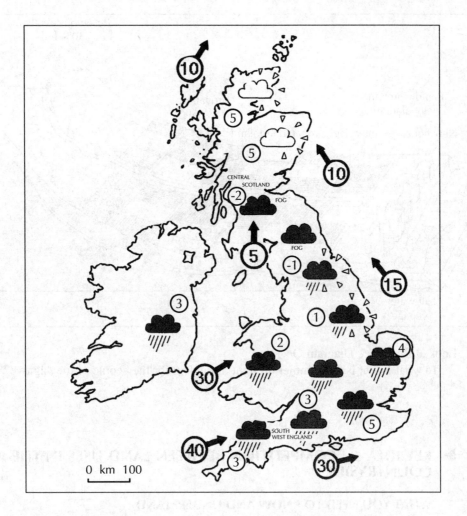

Look at Reference Map Q2.

In which area – central Scotland or south-west England – do you think the weather presents the greater number of problems? Give reasons for your answer. (ES, 4)

GENERAL LEVEL QUESTIONS

3   *Reference Diagram Q3: Land uses across the Inn Valley, Austria*

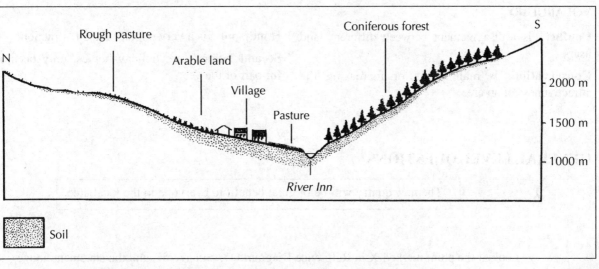

Explain the pattern of land use shown in Reference Diagram Q3. (KU, 5)

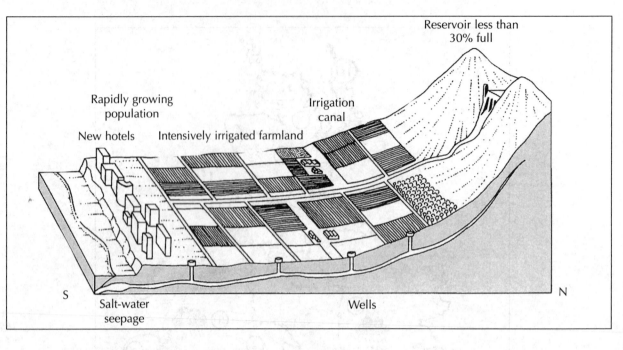

Look at Reference Diagram Q4.
  To what extent is the summer drought a problem for the people of the Algarve?   (ES, 6)

▶ **KEY IDEA 5   COMPETITION BETWEEN LAND USES IN THE COUNTRYSIDE**

WHAT YOU NEED TO KNOW AND UNDERSTAND

You need to know about the following:

1 The main land uses in the Scottish countryside, e.g. farming, forestry, recreation, water supply, quarrying.
2 The benefits that these land uses may bring to a rural area.
3 The problems that these land uses may create.

VOCABULARY

Conflict is a disagreement between different land users.

Conservation is maintaining or increasing the attractiveness of an area.

Honey-pot is a very popular tourist attraction.

Second homes are holiday homes, only occupied for part of the year.

GENERAL LEVEL QUESTIONS

1

> 'The new quarry will be of great benefit to everyone in the local area.'

Look at the point marked X in Reference Diagram Q1, on page 57, and the statement above.
  Do you agree with the statement above? Give reasons for your answer.   (ES, 4)

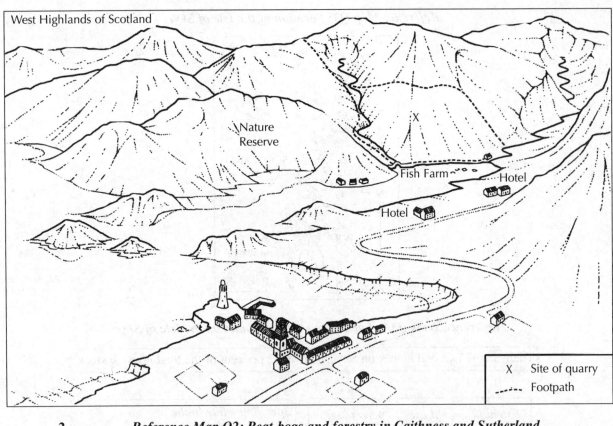

2   *Reference Map Q2: Peat-bogs and forestry in Caithness and Sutherland*

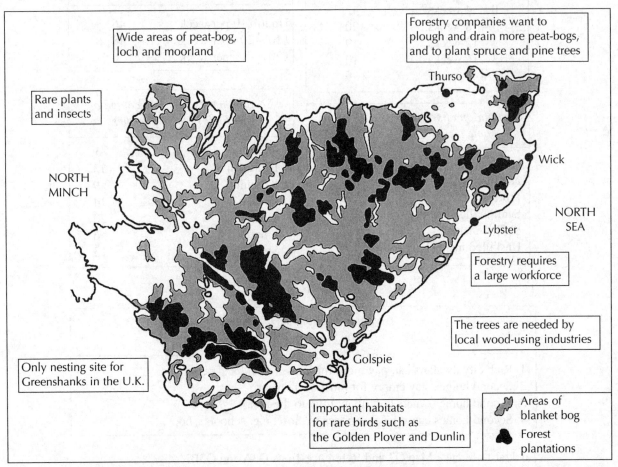

Look at Reference Map Q2 above. Do you think that more forests should be
planted in Caithness and Sutherland? Give reasons for your answer.

(ES, 4)

3
Reference Map Q3: Location of the Isle of Skye

Reference Texts Q3A: Facts about second homes on the Isle of Skye

There are 375 second homes on Skye. This is 12 per cent of the total housing stock.

Extent of annual use	(percentage)
0 – 4 weeks	42
5 – 8 weeks	20
9 – 12 weeks	19
13 – 16 weeks	10
17 + weeks	9

Spending while in the second home	(percentage)
Up to £10 per week	46
£10 – 20 per week	48
£20+ per week	6

Occupation of second home owner	(percentage)
Employer/manager	10
Non-manual	17
Professional	50
Semi-skilled manual	6
Skilled manual	17
Unskilled manual	0

Second homes as a percentage of the total in Skye parishes	
Bracadale	5
Duirinish	13
Kilmuir	9
Portree	14
Sleat	20
Snizort	6
Strath	13

Reference Text Q3B

Complaints about second homes on the Isle of Skye
1 Rich city dwellers can pay more for houses than local people.
2 Second homes stay empty for most of the year.
3 Second home owners contribute little to the area.
4 Second homes cause local services to close, e.g. schools, shops.

Look at Reference Map Q3 and Reference Texts Q3A and Q3B.

To what extent are the complaints about second homes on the Isle of Skye justified?

(ES, 6)

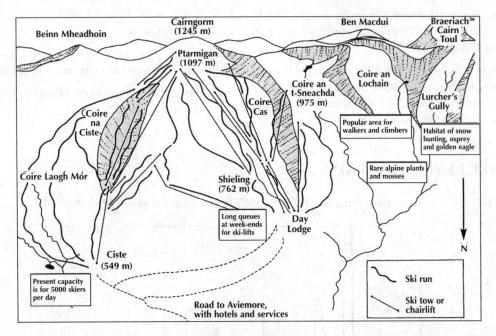

Reference Text Q4

> In the 1980s the Cairngorm Chairlift Company wanted to extend skiing into Lurcher's Gully. This would mean building a 2 km road, new car parks, more ski lifts and it would allow 4000 more skiers per day to enjoy the Cairngorms.

Look at Reference Diagram Q4 and Reference Text Q4. Describe the different points of view people would have towards the skiing development in Lurcher's Gully.

(ES, 6)

▶ KEY IDEA 6   THE THREAT TO DIFFERENT ENVIRONMENTS FROM HUMAN ACTIVITIES

WHAT YOU NEED TO KNOW AND UNDERSTAND

You need to know about the following:

1 The reasons why tropical forests are threatened.
2 The effects of cutting down tropical forests.
3 The ways in which deforestation can be controlled.
4 The reasons why tropical deserts are spreading.
5 The effects of the spread of deserts.
6 The ways in which the spread of deserts can be controlled.
7 The ways in which oceans become polluted.
8 The effects of ocean pollution.
9 The ways in which ocean pollution can be reduced.

VOCABULARY

Afforestation   is the planting of trees.

Debt for nature   is a scheme in which a country agrees to protect its environment in return for not having to repay the debts it owes to developed countries.

Deforestation   is the cutting down of trees.

Desertification   is the process by which farmland is turned into desert.

Food chain   is a series of organisms dependent upon one another for food.

Global warming   is the gradual rise in temperatures worldwide.

Greenhouse effect   is the gradual rise in temperature due to an increase in carbon dioxide and other gases in the atmosphere.

Overpopulation is where too many people live in an area for the resources available, resulting in a low standard of living.

Ozone layer is a belt 25–40 km above the earth's surface which absorbs most of the sun's ultra-violet rays. It is being destroyed by the release of chloro-fluoro-carbons (CFCs) into the atmosphere.

Pollution is the harmful effect of human activities on the environment.

Shelter belt is a line of trees which reduces windspeed and thereby protects the crops and soil behind it.

Soil erosion is the removal of soil by wind or rain.

GENERAL LEVEL QUESTIONS

1

Reference Diagram Q1: Rainfall in the Sahel region (1950–84)

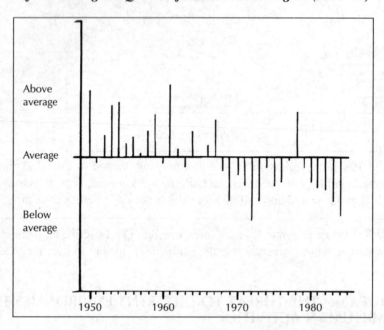

Reference Map Q1: The Sahel region of Africa

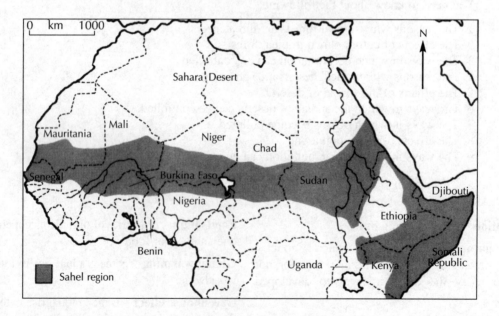

Look at Reference Diagram Q1 and Reference Map Q1.
(a) Describe the pattern of rainfall in the Sahel since 1950. (ES, 3)
(b) Explain in what ways lower rainfall in the Sahel can lead to desertification. (KU, 4)

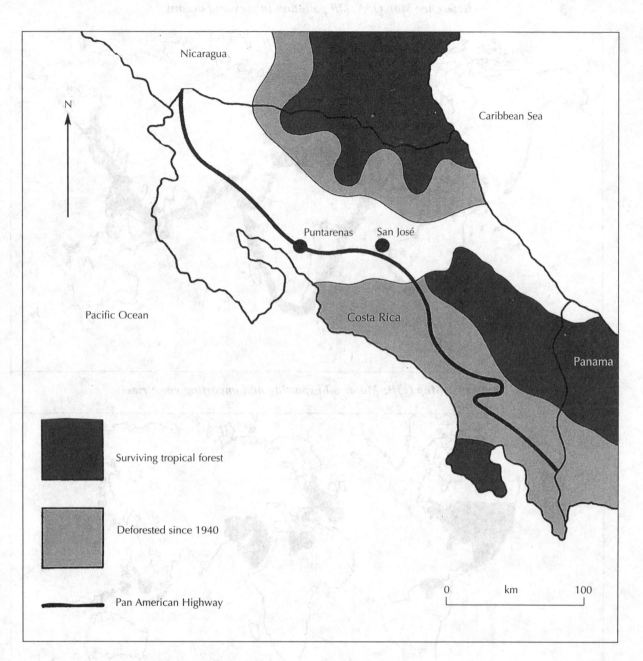

Reference Map Q2: Rainforest in Costa Rica

Legend:
- Surviving tropical forest
- Deforested since 1940
- Pan American Highway

(a) Look at Reference Map Q2.
 Compare the amount of tropical forest in Costa Rica in 1940 and 1990.   (ES, 2)

Reference Text Q2: Methods of reducing deforestation

1 Debt for nature
Costa Rica is protecting up to 15 per cent of its rainforests as National Parks. In return, it does not have to pay back the debts it owes some other countries. This gives it money for other developments.

2 Agro-forestry
The Inter-American Development Bank is funding agro-forestry in Costa Rica. Crops and trees are grown together. The trees provide fuel and keep the soil fertile, allowing higher yields from the crops beneath them.

(b) Look at Reference Text Q2. Two methods of reducing deforestation are described.
 Which method should Costa Rica use? Give reasons for your answer.   (ES, 4)

3   *Reference Map Q3A: Oil pollution in seas and oceans*

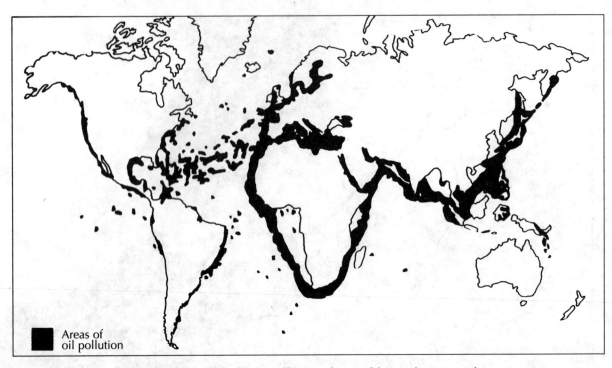

Areas of
oil pollution

Reference Map Q3B: Major oil exporting and importing countries

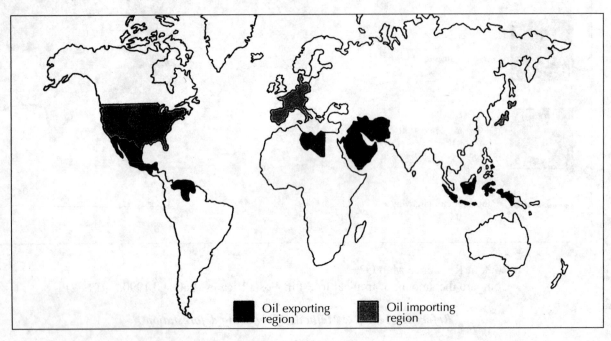

Oil exporting
region

Oil importing
region

(a) Describe the relationship between the information shown in Reference Maps Q3A and Q3B. (ES, 3)

Major sources of ocean pollution	
Transport	Farming
Industry	Domestic

(b) Which of the four major sources of ocean pollution is the easiest to control?
Give reasons for your answer. (ES, 4)

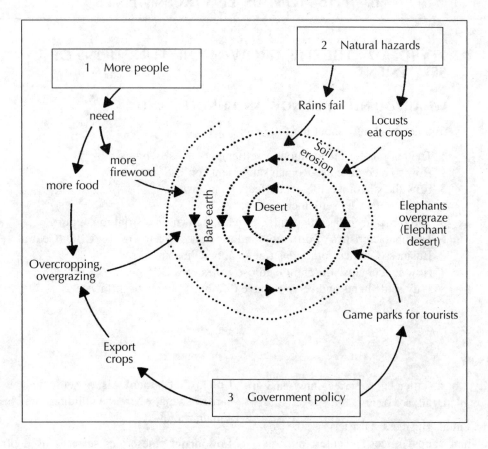

1   More people

need

more firewood

more food

Overcropping, overgrazing

Export crops

2   Natural hazards

Rains fail

Locusts eat crops

Soil erosion

Bare earth

Desert

Elephants overgraze (Elephant desert)

Game parks for tourists

3   Government policy

'Desertification is due almost entirely to natural factors.'

Look at Reference Diagram Q4 and the statement.
    To what extent is the statement true?   (ES, 6)

B THE HUMAN ENVIRONMENT

▶ KEY IDEA 7   THE SITE, GROWTH AND FUNCTIONS OF A SETTLEMENT

WHAT YOU NEED TO KNOW AND UNDERSTAND

You need to know about the following:

1 The reasons for the location of settlements in early times.
2 How to recognise pre-Roman settlements on O.S. maps.
3 How the site of a settlement affects its growth.
4 The reasons why settlements grow.
5 The functions of a settlement, e.g. market town, industrial town, port.
6 The characteristics of different land use zones in a town, e.g. CBD (Central Business District), old industrial area, new housing area.
7 How to recognise different land use zones on a O.S. map.
8 Why settlements and services have different spheres of influence.

VOCABULARY

Accessibility   of a settlement describes how easy it is to reach by road, rail, sea or air.

CBD   (or Central Business District) is the town centre, containing shops, offices and entertainments.

Conurbation   is a very large built-up area, formed when several towns merge together.

Dispersed   describes the settlement pattern in which buildings are scattered and not grouped together.

Dry-point   is a settlement on higher ground above a low-lying area with poor drainage.

Functions   of a settlement are the activities that take place there, e.g. providing services, port activity, and so on.

High order   describes services used rarely by most people and only found in towns and cities, e.g. an opera house, an international airport.

Land use zones   in a town are the areas of housing, industry and commerce (shops, offices, etc.).

Linear settlement   is a settlement with a long, narrow shape, where the buildings are clustered along a main routeway.

Low order   describes services used often by most people and found in most villages as well as in towns, e.g. post office, general store.

Nucleated   describes the settlement pattern in which the buildings are clustered together in the form of villages and towns.

Service centre   is a settlement which provides services for the local people.

Site   of a settlement is the land on which the settlement is built.

Sphere of influence   is the area around a settlement within which people use that settlement for its services.

Urban model   is a diagram showing a simplified pattern of land uses in a town.

1   *Reference Maps Q1: Two housing areas in Hawick, Scotland*

Area X

Area Y

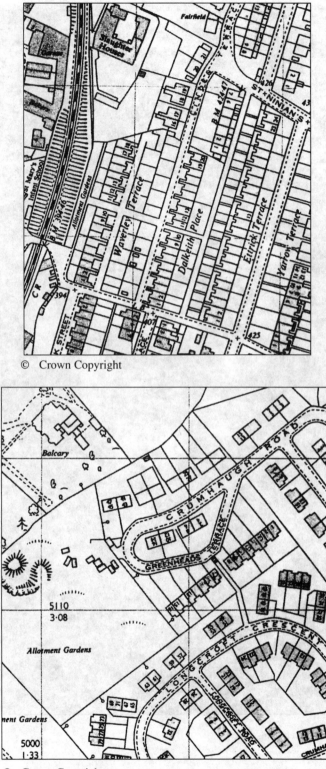

© Crown Copyright

© Crown Copyright

Look at Reference Maps Q1 which show the street patterns in two areas of Hawick.

(a) Which of the areas (X or Y) shows an old housing area? Give reasons for your answer.

(KU, 3)

(b) In what ways would a new industrial area differ from an old industrial area in a town?

(KU, 4)

Reproduced by kind permission of Aerofilms Ltd.

Look at the photograph.
  (a) Explain why Durham was a suitable site for a settlement in early times.   (KU, 4)
  (b) Explain why Durham found it difficult to grow in later years.   (KU, 2)

CREDIT LEVEL QUESTIONS

3　　　　*Reference Diagram Q3A: Land uses in a town*

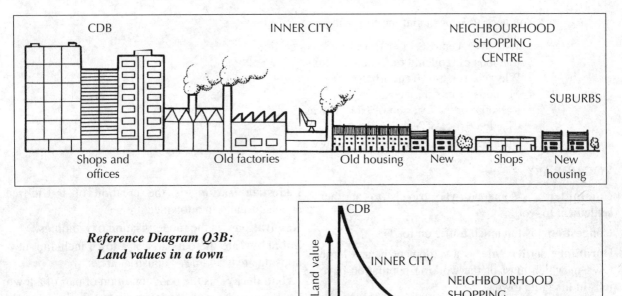

Reference Diagram Q3B: Land values in a town

Look at Reference Diagrams Q3A and Q3B.
(a) Describe the relationship between land use, land value and building height along the transect shown in Reference Diagram Q3A. (ES, 4)
(b) Explain the relationship between land use and land value in a town. (KU, 6)

4　　　　*Reference Map Q4: The location of Salisbury*

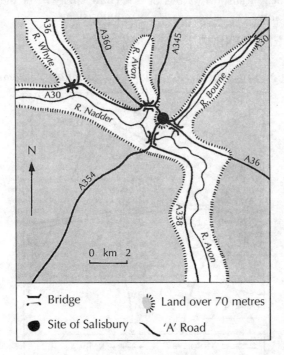

Look at Reference Map Q4.
(a) Explain fully why Salisbury is a route-centre. (KU, 3)
(b) Explain the functions a route-centre is likely to have. (KU, 3)

▶ KEY IDEA 8   RECENT CHANGES IN TOWNS AND CITIES

WHAT YOU NEED TO KNOW AND UNDERSTAND

You need to know about the following:

1 Why town centres suffer from traffic congestion.
2 Methods of reducing traffic congestion.
3 Why towns suffer from urban decay.
4 Methods of urban renewal.
5 Reasons for the location of New Towns.
6 Characteristics of New Towns.
7 Changes in land use at the edge of towns.

VOCABULARY

Commuter   is someone who travels to another settlement to work.

Congestion   is too much traffic on roads.

Dormitory settlement   is a settlement near a large town in which most of the working population have jobs in the large town.

Green Belt   is an area of countryside around a town in which new development is strictly controlled.

Inner city   is the old, central area of a town or city, including the CBD, the old industrial areas and old housing areas.

Neighbourhood   is a housing area in a town, usually a New Town.

Overspill   is a name for the population forced to move out of an area because of an urban renewal scheme.

Park 'n' ride   is a system in which car parks are set up at the edge of town and cheap transport by bus or rail is provided to the town centre.

Pedestrianisation   is the creation of traffic-free streets, usually in a town centre.

Renovation   is the modernisation of buildings.

Suburbs   are the outskirts of a town including new housing areas and new industrial areas.

Urban decay   is the poor condition of part of a town (its houses, shops, factories, transport facilities, etc.).

Urban fringe   is the zone at the edge of a town where it meets the countryside.

Urban redevelopment   is an urban renewal scheme in which buildings are pulled down and replaced by others (especially in the 1960s by high-rise flats).

Urban regeneration   is an urban renewal scheme involving improvements to housing, jobs, leisure and environment, so that the whole area receives a boost.

Urban renewal   is the name given to any improvement scheme to the condition of a town.

Urban sprawl   is the spreading of towns into the countryside.

GENERAL LEVEL QUESTIONS

 1

Reference Map Q1: Location of a dormitory settlement

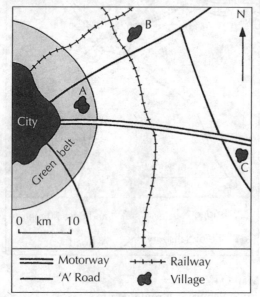

Look at Reference Map Q1.

(a) Which settlement (A, B or C) is most likely to become a dormitory settlement? Give reasons for your answer.   (ES, 3)

(b) New industries and hypermarkets are often built on the edges of towns. Give reasons why.   (KU, 4)

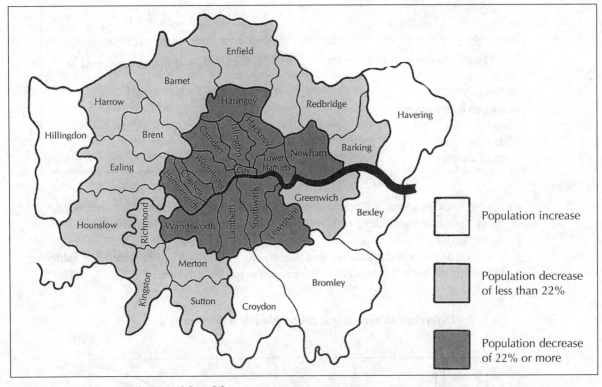

Look at Reference Map Q2.

(a) Describe the changes in population in London between 1971 and 1981. (ES, 3)

(b) Explain the disadvantages of living in an inner-city area. (KU, 4)

CREDIT LEVEL QUESTIONS

3　　　　　　　　　　*Reference Diagram Q3: Cartoon*

(a) Look at Reference Diagram Q3. It is a cartoon about the demolition of a block of high-rise flats. Explain fully why the women in the cartoon are pleased. (KU, 4)

Scheme X	Scheme Y
Buildings and docks converted to: offices expensive apartments hotel museum tourist shops.	Buildings and docks converted to: light industries leisure centre starter homes superstore.

(b) An old dockland area in Britain is undergoing urban regeneration. It is surrounded by nineteenth-century housing of former dockworkers, many of whom are now unemployed.

   Which of the urban regeneration schemes (X or Y) described in Reference Tables Q3 would be better for this area? Give reasons for your answer.   (ES, 5)

4   *Reference Diagram Q4: Street plan of a town centre*

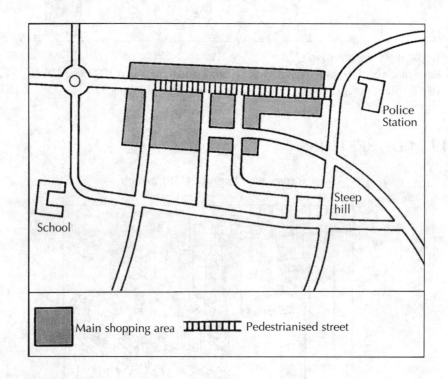

(a) The shopping area of the town shown in Reference Diagram Q4 suffers from traffic congestion.

   Describe the advantages and disadvantages of pedestrianising the main shopping street.   (ES, 6)

(b) Several cities in Europe charge motorists to enter the city centre.

   Do you think this is a suitable way of reducing traffic congestion? Give reasons for your answer.   (ES, 3)

WHAT YOU NEED TO KNOW AND UNDERSTAND

You need to know about the following:

1 The characteristics of arable, pastoral and mixed farms, especially their inputs, processes and outputs.
2 Reasons for the location of arable, pastoral and mixed farms.
3 How farm inputs have changed over the years.
4 The influence of the Government and the European Union on farming.
5 The ways in which farmers can earn additional income.
6 Reasons for the pattern of land use on farms.

VOCABULARY

Agribusiness is a very large farm in which huge sums of money are invested in buildings, machinery, chemicals, etc.

Arable farm is one in which most of the income is from crops.

Break crop is a crop used within a crop rotation system to maintain the fertility of the soil.

Cash crop is a crop grown for sale.

Casual workers are those employed only for a certain period during a year, e.g. at harvest time.

Cereal crop is a grain crop.

Common Agricultural Policy (CAP) is the European Union's policy on farming, designed to ensure that farmers earn enough money by offering guaranteed prices.

Co-operatives are groups of farmers who join together in order to get benefits, e.g. buying in bulk, sharing machinery.

Crofting is part-time mixed or livestock farming in Northern Scotland.

Crop rotation is where the crops are grown in different fields after a period of one year or more.

Diversification is the branching out into a different way of earning income.

Extensive farm is a farm with few inputs for its area, e.g. upland sheep farming.

Factory farming is the very intensive rearing of animals, often indoors, e.g. chickens.

Fodder crop is a crop given to animals to eat.

Grain crop is a crop whose grain is used, e.g. rice, wheat, oats.

Guaranteed price is the minimum price set by the European Community at which farmers can sell their produce.

Horticulture is the intensive cultivation of flowers, fruit and vegetables.

Inputs are what are needed in order to farm, e.g. land, labour, equipment.

Intensive farm is a farm with high inputs for its area, e.g. market gardening.

Ley pasture is pasture in a crop rotation system which will be ploughed up in a few years.

Market gardening is a small farm in which the produce is sent directly to market, e.g. flowers, vegetables.

Mixed farm is one in which the farmer earns money from crops and animals.

Monoculture is the growing of just one crop on a farm.

Organic farming is a method of farming which does not use chemicals as fertilisers or as pesticides.

Outputs are what the farmer produces, e.g. wheat, lambs, eggs.

Pastoral farm is one in which most of the income is from animals.

Permanent pasture is land always used as pasture.

Process is an activity done by the farmer in order to grow crops or rear animals, e.g. ploughing, milking.

Root crop is a crop whose root is used, e.g. potatoes, turnips, carrots.

Rough grazing is poor quality grazing land.

Standard man days are the number of days' work in a year that a farm animal or crop requires.

Under contract is a system by which crops are grown under a contract between the farmer and a processing company, especially sugar beet, peas.

71

1   *Reference Map QIA: Relief and cities in Scotland*

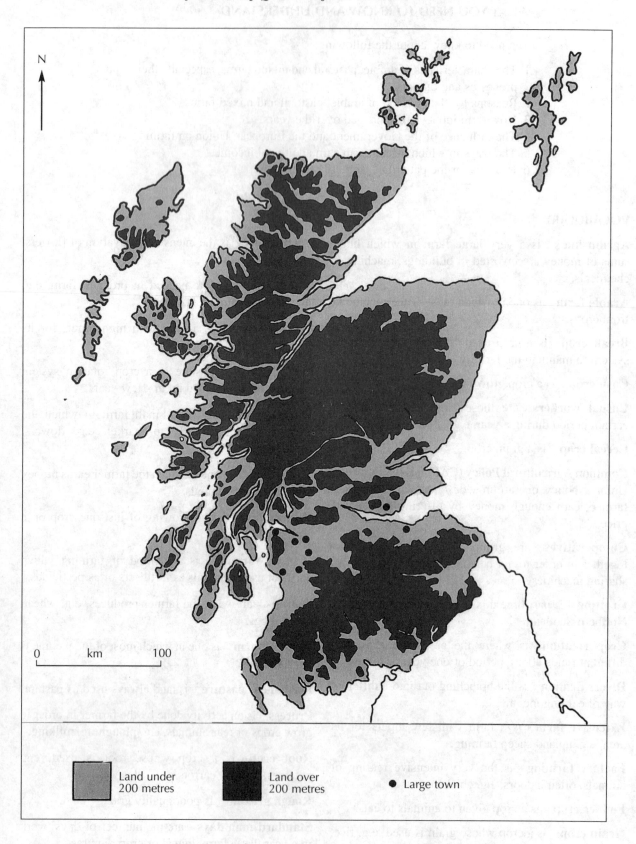

N

0   km   100

Land under
200 metres

Land over
200 metres

● Large town

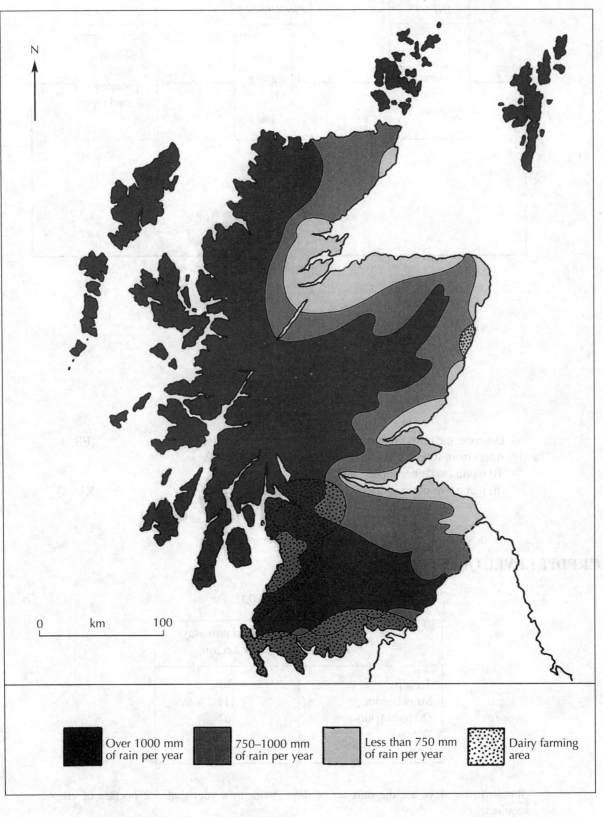

N

Over 1000 mm of rain per year	750–1000 mm of rain per year	Less than 750 mm of rain per year	Dairy farming area

0   km   100

Look at Reference Maps Q1A and Q1B.

(a) Describe the distribution of dairy farming in Scotland.   (ES, 3)

(b) Give reasons for the location of dairy farms in Scotland.   (KU, 4)

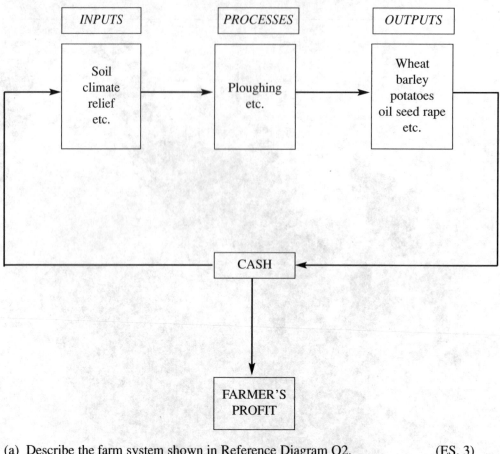

(a) Describe the farm system shown in Reference Diagram Q2.   (ES, 3)
(b) Apart from those mentioned in Reference Diagram Q2
   (i) name two other inputs, and
   (ii) name two other processes on an arable farm in the U.K.   (KU, 4)

CREDIT LEVEL QUESTIONS

3   *Reference Table Q3*

Crop	Standard man days per hectare
Turnips	30
Strawberries	111
Orchard fruits	62
Wheat	7
Grass	5

Standard man days are the number of days' work in a year that one hectare of crops requires.

(a) Explain how the information in Reference Table Q3 affects the pattern of land use on a farm.   (KU, 3)
(b) Explain the other factors which also influence the pattern of land use on a farm.
                                                                       (KU, 6)

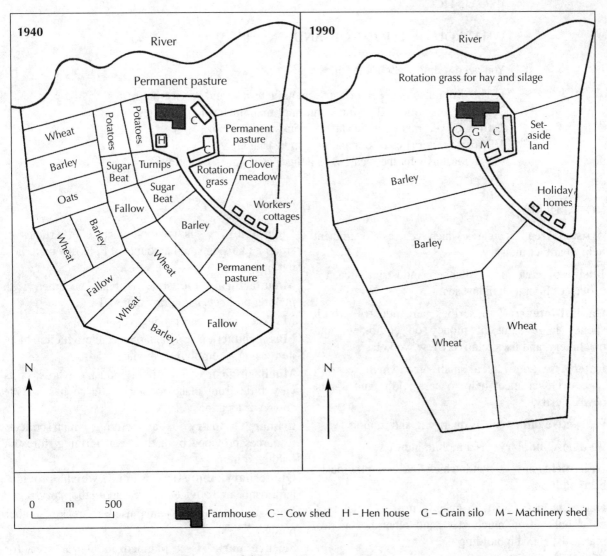

1940

River

Permanent pasture

Wheat

Potatoes

Potatoes

C

Permanent pasture

Barley

Sugar Beat

Turnips

Rotation grass

Clover meadow

H

C

Oats

Sugar Beat

Fallow

Barley

Workers' cottages

Wheat

Barley

Wheat

Fallow

Permanent pasture

Fallow

Wheat

Barley

Fallow

N

1990

River

Rotation grass for hay and silage

G C

M

Set-aside land

Barley

Holiday homes

Barley

Wheat

Wheat

N

0   m   500

Farmhouse   C – Cow shed   H – Hen house   G – Grain silo   M – Machinery shed

Look at Reference Diagrams Q4.

(a) Describe the ways in which the inputs and outputs on Monkton Farm have changed
     since 1940.   (ES, 5)

(b) Give reasons why the farm's inputs have changed.   (KU, 4)

WHAT YOU NEED TO KNOW AND UNDERSTAND

You need to know about the following:

1 The difference between primary, manufacturing, and service industries.
2 The factors which affect the location of manufacturing industries.
3 How Government policies affect industrial location.
4 The characteristics of old and new industrial areas.
5 The reasons why the location of industries changes over time.

VOCABULARY

Assisted Area   is an area which receives Government help to attract industry.

Business park   is a planned industrial area for offices or high tech industries.

Capital-intensive   describes an industry which spends large sums of money on equipment and machinery, and uses relatively few workers.

Enterprise zone   is a small area which receives special Government help to create jobs and attract new industry.

Extractive industry   is quarrying and mining.

Footloose industry   is a mobile industry.

Greenfield site   is land which has not previously been built on.

Heavy industry   is the manufacture of articles of great bulk using much steel and other heavy raw materials, e.g. shipbuilding.

High tech industry   is one which uses advanced equipment to produce goods.

Industrial estate   is a planned industrial area, often with ready-made factory units.

Industrial inertia   is the tendency of an industry to remain in an area when the original reason for its location has now gone.

Labour-intensive   describes an industry which requires a large workforce and relatively little capital equipment.

Light industry   is the manufacture of articles of small bulk using small amounts of light raw materials, e.g. jewellery.

Manufacturing industry   is one concerned with making products using raw materials.

Market   is where a product is sold.

Mass production   is the large-scale production of an item using assembly line methods.

Mobile industry   is a light industry whose costs vary little from place to place, and so has a wide choice of locations.

Primary industry   is an activity which collects resources provided by nature, e.g. farming, forestry, fishing, mining.

Quaternary industry   is one which provides information and advice, e.g. research laboratory.

Raw materials   are items used to make another product.

Science park   is a planned industrial area for industries concerned with research and advice.

Secondary industry   is a manufacturing industry.

Service industry   provides a service to people or other industries, e.g. transport, professions, administration, trades.

Sunrise industry   is the name given to new, growing industries, e.g. electronics in the U.K.

Sunset industry   is an old declining industry, e.g. shipbuilding in the U.K.

Tertiary industry   is a service industry.

1

Reference Diagram Q1A: Location of the chemical industry on Teesside in 1919

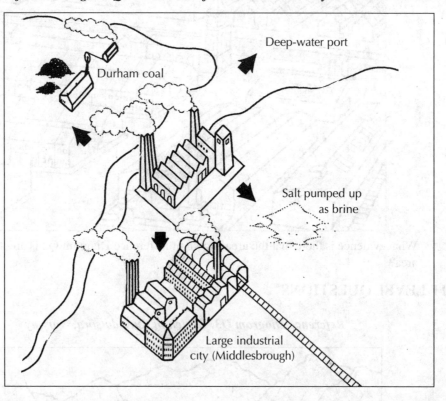

Reference Diagram Q1B: Location of the chemical industry on Teesside in 1993

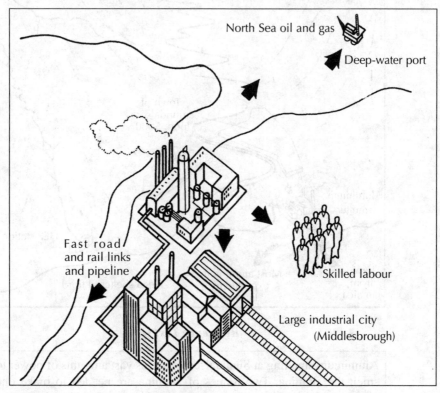

Look at Reference Diagrams Q1A and Q1B.

(a) Which three factors were most important in the location of the chemical industry on Teesside in 1919? (KU, 3)

(b) Some of the reasons why the industry located on Teesside have now gone.

Explain why the chemical industry remains on Teesside. (ES, 3)

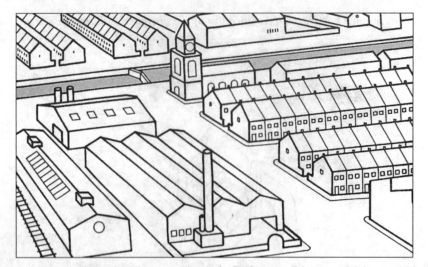

What evidence is there that the area shown in Reference Diagram Q2 is an old industrial area?   (KU, 4)

CREDIT LEVEL QUESTIONS

3   *Reference Diagram Q3: Sketch of Sunndalsora, Norway*

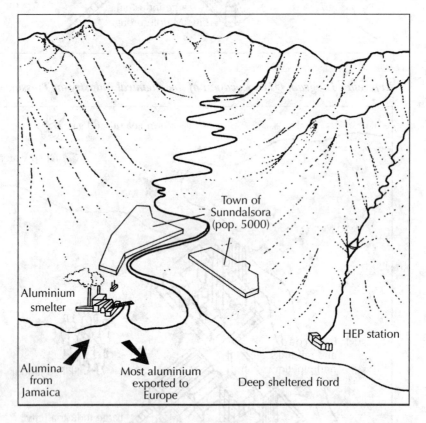

Reference Text Q3

> Aluminium smelting at Sunndalsora requires vast amounts of power to smelt the alumina. Two tonnes of alumina are needed to make one tonne of finished aluminium. The plant employs 1300 workers.

Look at Reference Diagram Q3 and Reference Text Q3.

Do you think Sunndalsora is a suitable location for an aluminium smelter? Give reasons for your answer.   (ES, 5)

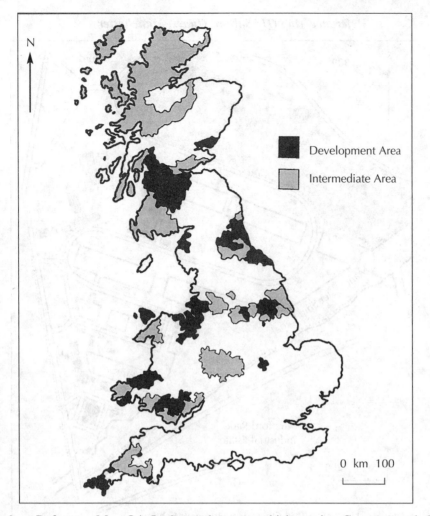

Look at Reference Map Q4. It shows the areas which receive Government help to attract industry.

(a) Describe the ways in which the Government can help to attract industry to an area of high unemployment.   (KU, 4)

(b) Which type of industry – heavy or light – is more likely to be attracted to an Assisted Area? Give reasons for your answer.   (ES, 4)

▶ **KEY IDEA 11   THE EFFECTS OF AN INDUSTRY OPENING OR CLOSING**

WHAT YOU NEED TO KNOW AND UNDERSTAND

You need to know about the following:

1 The effects of a new industry on employment, the local community, and the environment.

2 The effects of the closure of an industry on employment, the local community and the environment.

VOCABULARY

Derelict land   is land or the buildings on it which are disused and run-down.

Economic effects   are the financial effects on jobs and income.

Environmental effects   are the effects on the landscape and to the environment.

Multiplier effect   is the 'knock-on' effect of an industry opening or closing on other industries and services.

Restored land   is derelict land which is made useful again, e.g. by landscaping, renovating buildings.

Social effects   are the effects on the quality of life of the people, e.g. standard of living, services, community spirit.

1   *Reference Map Q1: Salford Quays, Manchester*

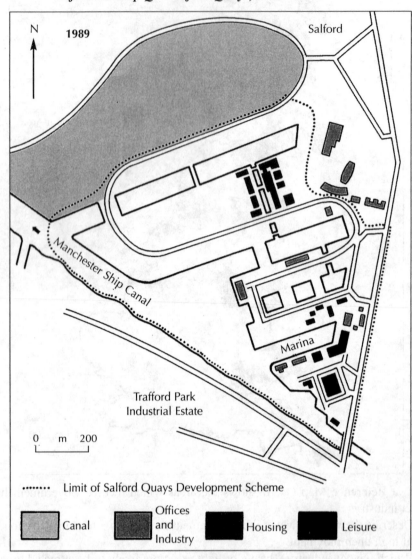

Reference Map Q1 legend:

.... Limit of Salford Quays Development Scheme

Canal   Offices and Industry   Housing   Leisure

Reference Tables Q1

Salford Quays in 1985	Salford Quays Development Scheme (started in 1988)
Old housing, mostly rented by local people Much unemployment amongst unskilled dock workers Widespread vandalism Decaying warehouses and docks	Construction work provided 4000 jobs Luxury homes built for sale New shopping and office complex New marina

'The social and economic effects of the Salford Quays Development Scheme will bring great benefits to the local people.'

Look at Reference Map Q1, Reference Tables Q1 and the statement.
Do you agree with the statement? Give reasons for your answer.   (ES, 4)

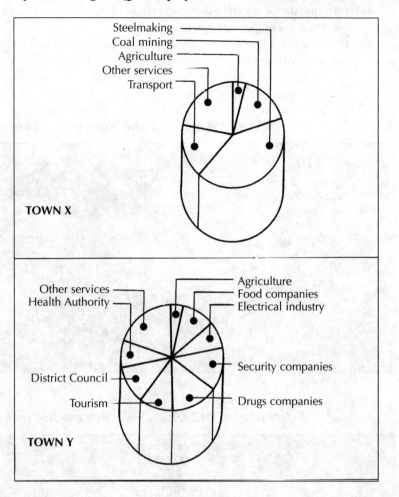

Steelmaking
Coal mining
Agriculture
Other services
Transport

TOWN X

Other services
Health Authority

Agriculture
Food companies
Electrical industry

Security companies

District Council

Tourism

Drugs companies

TOWN Y

Look at Reference Diagram Q2 which shows the employment pattern for two towns in Scotland.

(a) Compare the employment pattern of the two towns. (ES, 3)

(b) Which town will suffer more if an industry closes – town X or town Y? Give reasons for your answer. (ES, 3)

CREDIT LEVEL QUESTIONS

3 *Reference Map Q3: Major job losses in north-east England in 1998*

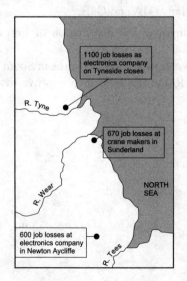

1100 job losses as electronics company on Tyneside closes

R. Tyne

670 job losses at crane makers in Sunderland

R. Wear

NORTH SEA

600 job losses at electronics company in Newton Aycliffe

R. Tees

Look at Reference Map Q3.

(a) Describe the social and economic effects of the closure of three major factories in north-east England in the same year. (KU, 5)

(b) Describe ways in which the Government can help areas affected by the sudden closure of major factories. (KU, 4)

4

Reference Map Q4A: South Wales ironworks in 1860

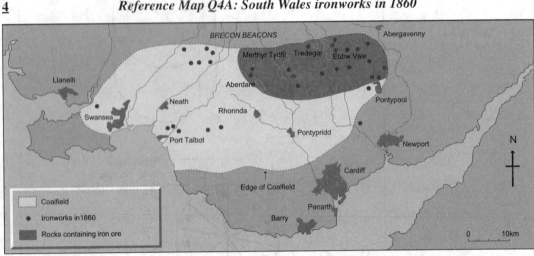

Reference Map Q4B: South Wales iron and steelworks in 1997

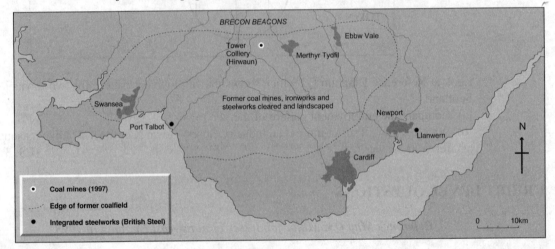

Look at Reference Maps Q4A and Q4B.

(a) Describe the changes in the distribution of iron and steelworks in South Wales since 1860. (ES, 3)

(b) Many coal mines and iron and steelworks in South Wales have closed in recent years. Do you think their closure has helped to improve the environment? Give reasons for your answer. (ES, 4)

C INTERNATIONAL ISSUES

▶ **KEY IDEA 12 THE WORLD DISTRIBUTION OF POPULATION**

WHAT YOU NEED TO KNOW AND UNDERSTAND

You need to know about the following:

1 Reasons why some regions have a high population density.
2 Reasons why some regions have a low population density.
3 That the population distribution in any area is affected by environmental, political, and economic factors.

VOCABULARY

Economic factors are those connected with money, industry, jobs, standard of living.

Empty lands are areas with a low population density.

Environmental factors are those connected with the natural environment e.g. climate, relief, soil.
Negative areas are regions with a low population density.
Political factors are those connected with Government and European Union decisions.

GENERAL LEVEL QUESTIONS

1   *Reference Map Q1: World density of population*

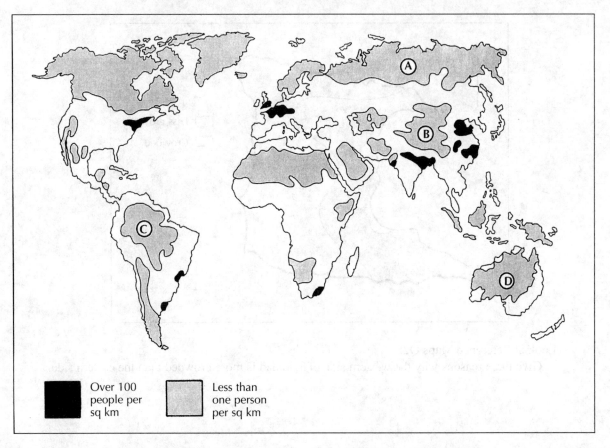

Choose two of the areas marked A, B, C and D on Reference Map Q1.
For each area you have chosen, give two reasons why the population density is low.

(KU, 4)

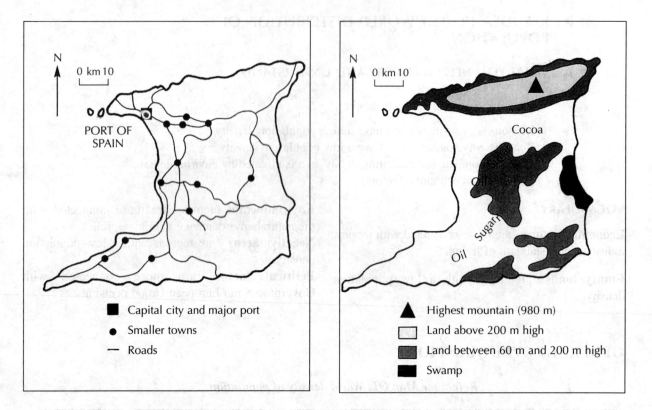

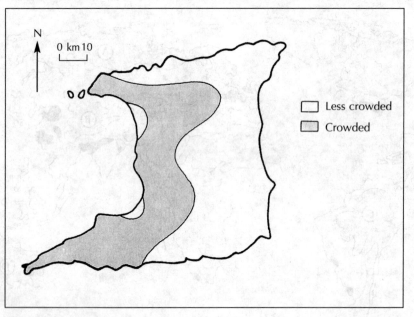

Look at Reference Maps Q2.

Give three reasons why the western side of Trinidad is more crowded than the eastern side.

(KU, 3)

3　　　　　　*Reference Maps Q3: Ghana, West Africa*

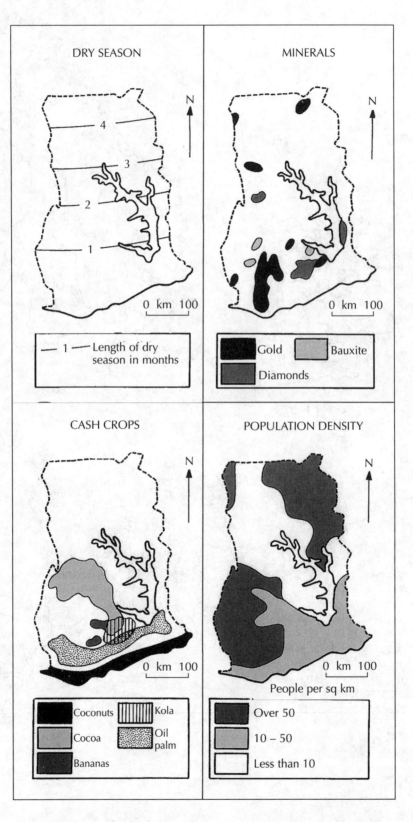

Describe the interrelationships between the distributions shown in Reference Maps Q3.

(ES, 6)

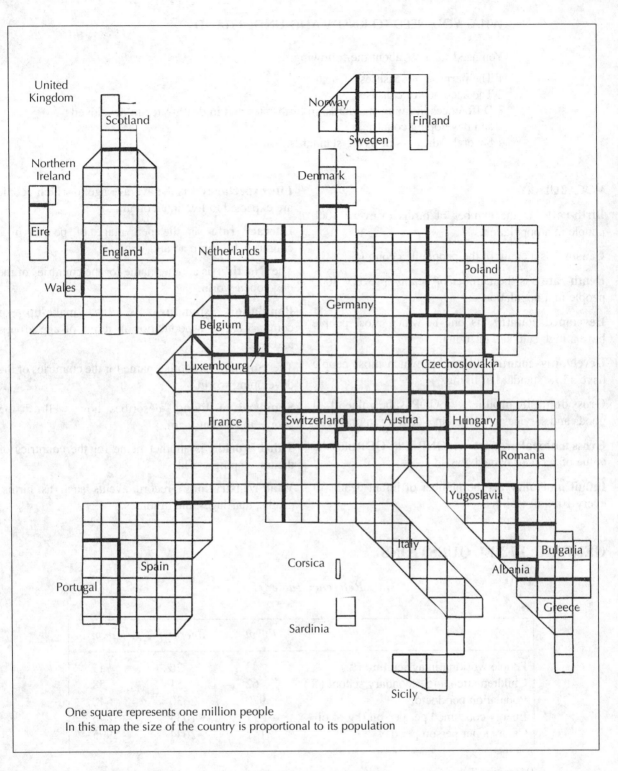

One square represents one million people
In this map the size of the country is proportional to its population

(a) Use Reference Maps Q4A and Q4B to describe variations in population density throughout Europe. (ES, 3)

(b) The population density of an area can be explained by environmental, political and economic factors.

Choose one environmental, one political, and one economic factor. Explain how each one can affect population density. (KU, 6)

► KEY IDEA 13   THE CHARACTERISTICS OF POPULATIONS

WHAT YOU NEED TO KNOW AND UNDERSTAND

You need to know about the following:

1 The purpose of censuses.
2 The accuracy of censuses.
3 Differences in living standards, in birth-rates and in death-rates in developed and developing countries.
4 Several indicators of living standards.

VOCABULARY

Birth-rate is the number of births to every 1000 people in a population.

Census is a count of the people in a country.

Death-rate is the number of deaths in every 1000 people in a population.

Developed country is one in which most people have a high standard of living.

Developing country is one in which most people have a low standard of living.

Gross domestic product or GDP is the value of all goods and services produced in a country in one year.

Gross national product or GNP is the GDP plus the value of services earned abroad.

Infant mortality is the number of infant deaths to every 1000 live births.

Life expectancy is the average age to which people are expected to live in a country.

Literacy rate is the percentage of people in a country who can read and write.

The '**North**' is another name for the countries of the developed world.

Population structure is the make-up or composition of a population in terms of age groups and sex.

The '**South**' is another name for the countries of the developing world.

Standard of living describes how well-off the people in a country are.

Third World is another name for the countries of the developing world.

Vital registrations record events such as births, deaths, marriages and divorces.

GENERAL LEVEL QUESTIONS

<u>1</u>   *Reference Table Q1*

	Egypt	Algeria	Lebanon
People working in agriculture (%)	43	26	11
Children attending secondary school (%)	62	51	58
Population per doctor	970	2630	540
Energy consumed per person (kg of oil)	577	1034	846
Calories per person per day	3157	2644	2995

Reference Table Q1 gives information on three developing countries.

Which of the three countries has the highest standard of living? Give three reasons for your answer.   (ES, 3)

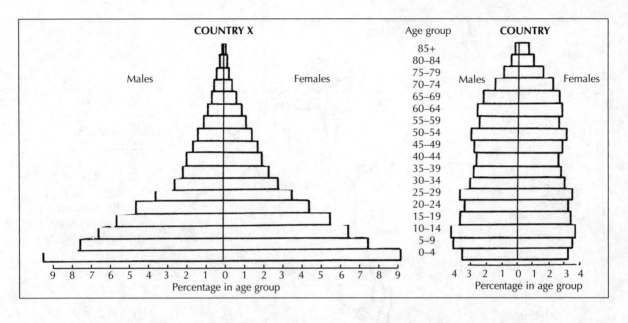

(a) What are the benefits to a country of taking a census?   (KU, 3)
(b) Look at Reference Diagrams Q2.
     Which country (X or Y) is a developing country? Give reasons for your answer.
                                                                   (KU, 2)

CREDIT LEVEL QUESTIONS

3   *Reference Diagram Q3: Life expectancy and literacy rates in selected countries*

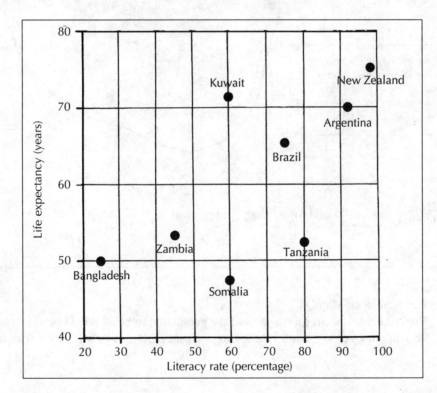

(a) Describe the relationship between life expectancy and literacy rate, as shown in
     Reference Diagram Q3.   (ES, 3)
(b) Describe the arguments for and against using life expectancy and literacy rate as
     indicators of standard of living.   (KU, 4)

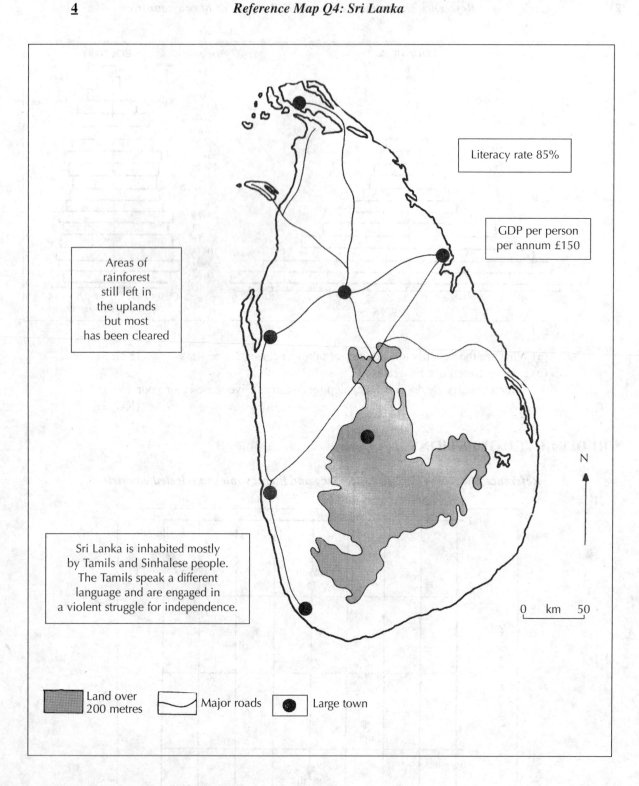

Literacy rate 85%

GDP per person
per annum £150

Areas of
rainforest
still left in
the uplands
but most
has been cleared

Sri Lanka is inhabited mostly
by Tamils and Sinhalese people.
The Tamils speak a different
language and are engaged in
a violent struggle for independence.

N

0   km   50

Land over
200 metres   Major roads   Large town

Look at Reference Map Q4.
   The last census in Sri Lanka showed the population to be 14 847 000.
   Do you think censuses in Sri Lanka are accurate? Give reasons for your answer.   (ES, 4)

WHAT YOU NEED TO KNOW AND UNDERSTAND

You need to know about the following:

1 How birth-rates, death-rates, and migration affect population growth.
2 Reasons why countries have different birth-rates and death-rates.
3 Reasons why birth-rates and death-rates change.
4 Reasons why people migrate within developed countries.
5 Reasons why people migrate within developing countries.
6 Reasons why people migrate from developing to developed countries.
7 Effects of a rapid increase in population on a city or country.
8 Effects of a decrease in population on a country.
9 Ways in which countries can slow down their population increase.
10 Ways in which countries can increase their populations.

VOCABULARY

Active population   is the number of people in a country of working age (usually 15–65 years).

Dependent population   is the number of people in a country who are not of working age (children and senior citizens).

Guest workers   are people allowed to live and work in another country for a short period of time.

Migration   is the movement of people from one area to another.

Natural increase   is the number of extra people in a population each year; the difference between the births and deaths.

Overpopulation   is where too many people live in an area for the resources available, resulting in a low standard of living.

Pull factor   is a reason which attracts people to migrate to another area, e.g. for higher education.

Push factor   is a reason why people move away from an area, e.g. unemployment.

Refugees   are people forced to move away from their home area.

Shanty town   is an area within a large town in which people have built makeshift houses on waste land; sometimes called squatter camps.

GENERAL LEVEL QUESTIONS

<u>1</u>   *Reference Diagram Q1: Population structure of Moroccan immigrants to France*

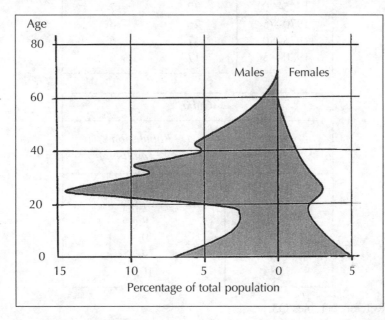

Look at Reference Diagram Q1.

(a) Describe the population characteristics of immigrants from Morocco to France.   (ES, 2)

(b) Explain why most immigrants have the characteristics you have described.   (KU, 2)

91

Reference Diagram Q2: The effects of China's growing population

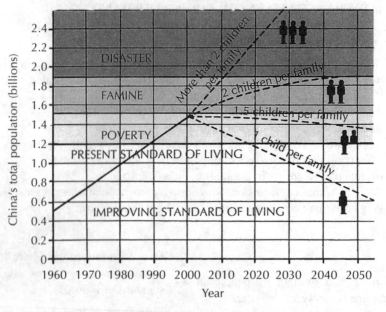

(a) Describe what Reference Diagram Q2 shows. (ES, 3)

(b) Describe ways in which countries such as China can reduce their birth-rates. (KU, 4)

CREDIT LEVEL QUESTIONS

3

Reference Tables Q3

Cuba		
Year	Birth-rate	Death-rate
1960–65	35	9
1965–70	32	7
1970–75	26	6
1975–80	17	6
1980–85	17	6

Cuba	
Year	Population Total (millions)
1960	6.9
1965	7.8
1970	8.6
1975	9.3
1980	9.7
1985	10.1

Look at Reference Tables Q3.

(a) Describe the relationship between birth-rate, death-rate and population growth in Cuba between 1960 and 1980. (ES, 3)

(b) Draw a single graph to show the information given in Reference Tables Q3. (KU, 4)

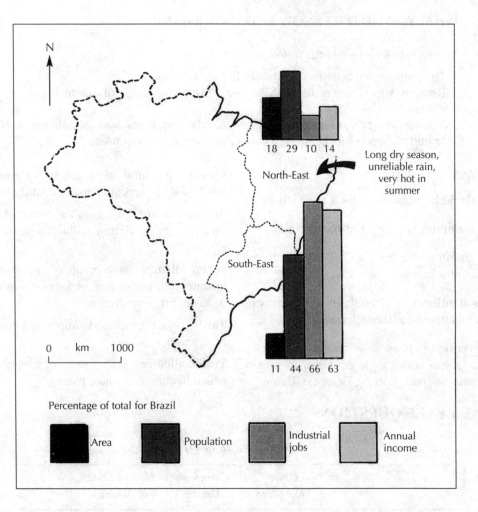

Reference Table Q4: Living standards in North-East and South-East Brazil

	North-East Brazil	South-East Brazil
Life expectancy	48 years	63 years
Infant mortality	19%	7%
Houses with clean water to drink	20%	78%
Houses with sewage disposal	25%	73%
Children aged 10–14 attending school	57%	83%

Look at Reference Map Q4 and Reference Table Q4.

Many people migrate from North-East Brazil to South-East Brazil.

Experts cannot agree whether the social, economic or environmental factors are the main reasons why the people migrate. Describe the arguments for all three points of view.

(ES, 6)

WHAT YOU NEED TO KNOW AND UNDERSTAND

You need to know about the following:

1 The purpose and benefits of alliances between countries.
2 Reasons why Europe, the U.S.A. and Japan have a lot of international influence.
3 That a country's influence on others may be due to its size, population, resources, level of technology, location, or historical connections.

VOCABULARY

Common Market   is the name for a trade alliance.

European Community   See **European Union**.

European Union   is a trade and social alliance of European countries.

International influence   is the ability of a country to affect other countries, e.g. through trade and aid.

Lomé Convention   is an agreement which allows African, Caribbean, and Pacific countries to import agreed amounts of goods into the European Union.

Quota   is a limit on the amount of goods a country is allowed to export to another country.

Selling alliance   is a group of countries which agree on a price at which they will sell a particular product, e.g. oil.

Social alliance   is a group of countries which co-operate with each other in various ways, e.g. sport, defence, aid, immigration.

Tariff   is a tax on goods imported into one country from another.

Trade alliance   is a group of countries between which free trade can take place.

GENERAL LEVEL QUESTIONS

1

Reference Table Q1

	United Kingdom	*European Union*	*United States of America*	*Japan*
Area (million sq km)	0.24	2	9	0.37
Population (millions)	57	323	242	121
GDP ($ million)	368	2217	3276	1184

Look at Reference Table Q1.

Describe how the United Kingdom has achieved greater international influence by being a member of the European Union alliance. (KU, 3)

2   *Reference Diagram Q2: World oil prices (1960–87)*

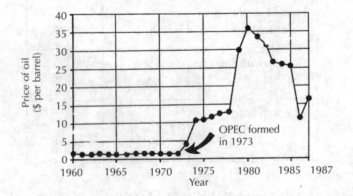

Look at Reference Diagram Q2.
(a) Describe the advantages of a selling alliance such as the Organisation of Petroleum Exporting Countries (OPEC). (KU, 2)
(b) Describe the changes in the price of oil before and after the formation of OPEC. (ES, 2)

CREDIT LEVEL QUESTIONS

3   *Reference Map Q3: The ECOWAS countries of West Africa*

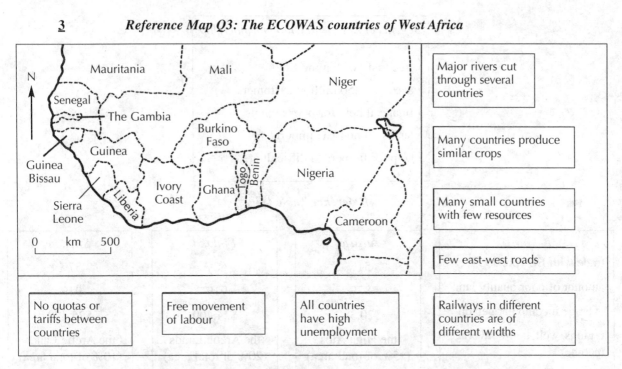

Look at Reference Map Q3.

(a) ECOWAS is a trade alliance between West African countries.

Describe the advantages of setting up a trade alliance such as ECOWAS. (KU, 4)

(b) Suggest reasons why ECOWAS has had little success so far.   (ES, 4)

4   *Reference Map Q4: The countries of the European Union*

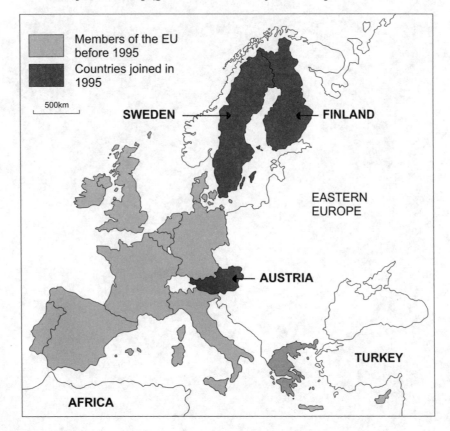

Benefits of European Union membership
• free trade within the EU
• access to 350 million customers
• financial help for poor regions
• tariffs on non-EU imports
• help for farmers in difficult areas

Reference Table Q4

	Austria	Finland	Sweden
trade with EU (pre-1995)	51%	60%	57%
amount of poor quality land	83%	91%	93%
average income per person	$20,380	$24,400	$25,490
regions well below average income	the High Alps (15% of total area)	the Arctic Lands (20% of total area)	the Arctic Lands (10% of total area)

Look at Reference Map Q4, Reference Text Q4 and Reference Table Q4.

In 1995 Austria, Finland and Sweden joined the European Union.

Which country would have benefited most from joining the EU? Give reasons for your answer. (ES, 5)

► KEY IDEA 16   INTERNATIONAL TRADE

WHAT YOU NEED TO KNOW AND UNDERSTAND

You need to know about the following:

1 The difference in trade patterns between developed and developing countries.
2 The interdependence of developed and developing countries in trade.
3 The ways in which the prices of primary and manufactured goods change.
4 The trade problems of developing countries, and possible solutions to these problems.
5 Barriers to world trade, e.g. quotas, tariffs.

VOCABULARY

Consumer   is a person, industry, or country that uses a product, e.g. the U.K. is a consumer of oil.

Countertrade   is a system whereby goods are exchanged between countries and no money is involved.

Exports   are goods sold to another country.

Imports   are goods bought from another country.

Manufactured goods   are goods that have been made from raw materials.

Multinational company   is a very large company which has operations in many different countries, e.g. General Motors.

Overproduction   of a product is when more is produced than can be sold, causing the price to fall.

Producer   is a person, industry, or country that produces something, e.g. Brazil is a producer of coffee.

Trade balance   is the difference between the value of a country's exports and imports.

Trade barrier   is an obstacle which restricts the amount of goods sold in another country, e.g. quota, tariff.

Trade deficit   is the amount by which the value of imports exceeds the value of exports.

Trade surplus   is the amount by which the value of exports exceeds the value of imports.

Transnational company   is another name for a multinational company.

GENERAL LEVEL QUESTIONS

1   *Reference Diagram Q1A: Imports and exports of a developing country*

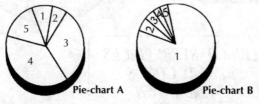

1 Raw materials
2 Chemicals
3 Manufactured goods
4 Machinery and transport equipment
5 Food, drink and tobacco

(a)   Pie-charts A and B in Reference Diagram Q1A show the imports and exports of a typical developing country. Which pie-chart (A or B) refers to the country's imports? Give reasons for your answer.   (KU, 2)

Reference Diagram Q1B: World price of tin (1976–87)

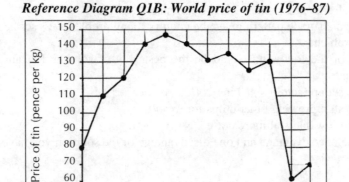

(b)   Look at Reference Diagram Q1B. Most of the world's tin comes from developing countries. Describe the effects of the changes in the world price of tin on the countries which export it.   (KU, 3)

97

Exports		Imports	
Commodity	*Percentage*	*Commodity*	*Percentage*
Coffee	54	Machinery	27
Cotton	17	Vehicles	8
Sisal	7	Textiles	11
Diamonds	5	Petroleum products	30
Cashew nuts	4	Iron and Steel	6
Others	13	Others	18
Total: $370 million	100	Total: $830 million	100

Reference Text Q2: Newspaper headlines

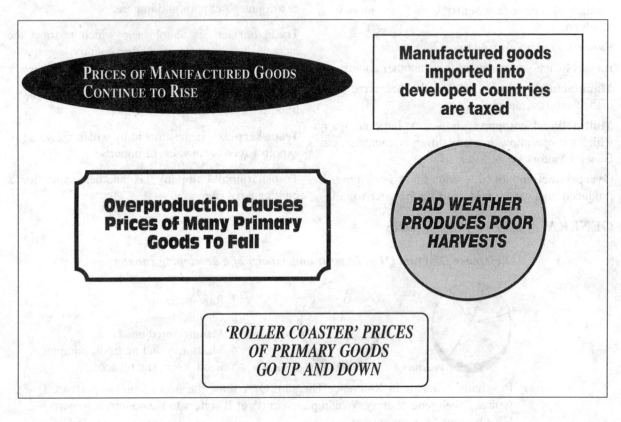

(a) Look at Reference Table Q2 and Reference Text Q2.

Tanzania's trade pattern gives the country many problems. Describe some of these problems. (KU, 4)

(b) Which of the following would be the best way of solving Tanzania's trade problem?

(i) To set up factories making coffee powder.

(ii) To start growing other crops for export.

(iii) To grow and sell more coffee.

Describe one advantage and one disadvantage of the solution you have chosen.

(ES, 4)

CREDIT LEVEL QUESTIONS

3   *Reference Table Q3*

Goods imported into the U.K.	U.K. Tariff (percentage)
Rice	0
Processed rice	13
Crude palm oil	4
Refined palm oil	12
Cocoa beans	0
Cocoa powder	30
Chocolate	35

Look at Reference Table Q3.

(a) Describe the variations in U.K. tariffs on imported goods.   (ES, 3)

(b) The U.K. and developing countries that supply these goods have different opinions about the tariffs. Describe the different opinions they have.   (ES, 4)

4 (a) In what ways are the developing and developed countries interdependent in trade?   (KU, 3)

(b) Look at Reference Tables Q4 below.

To what extent are the U.K. and Ghana interdependent in trade?   (ES, 4)

Reference Tables Q4: Trade between Ghana and the U.K.

Ghana's exports to the U.K.	£106m
Proportion of its total exports	27%

U.K.'s exports to Ghana	£126m
Proportion of its total exports	0.2%

Ghana's main exports	Percentage
Cocoa	67
Aluminium	10
Timber	6

U.K.'s main exports	Percentage
Crude oils	16
Machinery	15
Chemicals	12
Transport equipment	10
Food and drink	6
Metals	5

▶ KEY IDEA 17   INTERNATIONAL AID AND SELF-HELP

WHAT YOU NEED TO KNOW AND UNDERSTAND

You need to know about the following:

1 The reasons why international aid and self-help schemes are needed in developing countries.
2 The methods of giving aid, e.g. tied aid, voluntary aid.
3 The types of international aid, e.g. short-term aid, long-term aid.
4 The effects of international aid and self-help schemes.
5 The types of self-help schemes.

VOCABULARY

Appropriate technology is the use of equipment for developing a country most suited to the skills and finances of the local people.

Barefoot doctor is someone trained to recognise and treat local diseases and to offer medical advice.

Bilateral aid is aid from one country to another.

High technology is advanced equipment used to develop a country, e.g. large dams and reservoirs, power stations.

Intermediate technology is the use of equipment which is better than primitive, low technology but not as advanced as high technology. In developing countries it is often the most appropriate technology to use.

Long-term aid is aid which takes months or years before it benefits an area, e.g. new roads, forest plantations.

Low technology is the use of primitive techniques and equipment which are cheap and which work on a small scale, e.g. simple water-lifting devices for irrigation.

Multilateral aid is aid from a group of countries to an agency which then distributes it to other countries.

Official aid is bilateral or multilateral aid, from one or more countries to another.

Project aid is aid used for a large project, e.g. a hydro-electric power station, a large hospital.

Self-help scheme is a scheme which uses the skills of the local people in a country to improve conditions.

Short-term aid is emergency aid, needed after natural disasters such as floods, earthquakes.

Tied aid is aid with conditions attached, e.g. the money must be spent on goods from the country giving the aid.

United Nations is an organisation to which nearly all the countries of the world belong. It aims to improve conditions for people throughout the world.

Voluntary aid is aid given by the public to charities, which then distribute it where it is needed.

GENERAL LEVEL QUESTIONS

1   *Reference Text Q1*

> Bilateral aid (90 per cent of all aid) is given from one country to another. It is often tied aid. This means the aid is given for agreed projects, and equipment must be bought in the country giving the aid.
>
> Multilateral aid (7 per cent of all aid) is from a group of countries to an organisation, which then gives it to another country.
>
> Voluntary aid accounts for 3 per cent of all aid.

Look at Reference Text Q1.
(a) Give one example of:
   (i) a multilateral aid organisation. (ii) a voluntary aid organisation.   (KU, 2)
(b) Describe the advantages and disadvantages of tied aid to a developing country.
                       (KU, 4)

2   *Reference Text Q2A*

> # FLOOD DISASTER   *14 September 1987*
>
> **MORE than 24 million people in Bangladesh are either homeless or without food after the worst floods in the country's history.**
>
> Torrential rain is partly to blame, but the main problem is the torrent of water rushing down from the Himalayas. Deforestation here has doubled the amount of water and topsoil running off the Himalayas.
>
> The death toll is 1300 and many are still dying from disease. 3000 kilometres of road and 1200 bridges have been destroyed.
>
> Floods in Bangladesh are only too common. Next year the people will live in fear of yet another disastrous flood.

Look at Reference Text Q2A. It is a newspaper article describing a severe flood in Bangladesh.
(a) Explain the types of short-term aid that Bangladesh needed after this flood. (KU, 3)

Method A	Method B
All funds used on short-term aid for Bangladesh.	Half the funds spent on short-term aid. Half the funds spent on long-term aid for Bangladesh.

(b) Look at Reference Tables Q2B.

A charity organisation wishes to use some of its funds to help Bangladesh after the flood disaster. In what way should they spend their money – using Method A or Method B? Give reasons for your answer.   (ES, 3)

CREDIT LEVEL QUESTIONS

<u>3</u>   *Reference Diagram Q3A: Methods of cooking in developing country X*

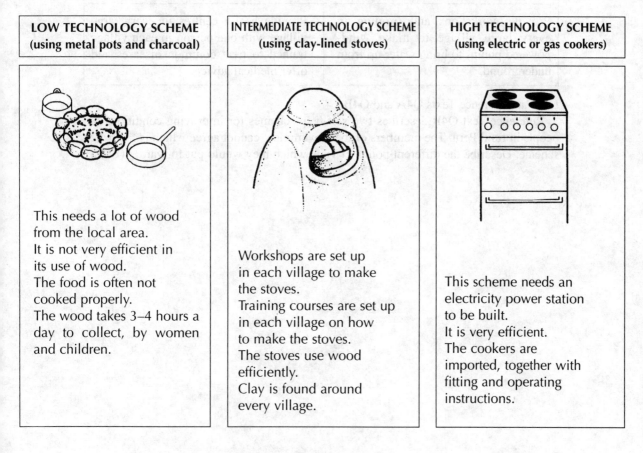

LOW TECHNOLOGY SCHEME (using metal pots and charcoal)	INTERMEDIATE TECHNOLOGY SCHEME (using clay-lined stoves)	HIGH TECHNOLOGY SCHEME (using electric or gas cookers)

This needs a lot of wood from the local area. It is not very efficient in its use of wood. The food is often not cooked properly. The wood takes 3–4 hours a day to collect, by women and children.

Workshops are set up in each village to make the stoves. Training courses are set up in each village on how to make the stoves. The stoves use wood efficiently. Clay is found around every village.

This scheme needs an electricity power station to be built. It is very efficient. The cookers are imported, together with fitting and operating instructions.

Reference Text Q3B: Data on developing country X

Literacy rate	27%
Unemployment	21%
Life expectancy	51 years

Look at Reference Diagram Q3A and Reference Text Q3B.

The people of developing country X mostly use low technology for cooking their food. The Government wishes to improve the methods of cooking used.

(a) Explain the disadvantages of using low technology methods for cooking.   (ES, 3)

(b) Describe the arguments for and against using intermediate technology methods and high technology methods.   (ES, 6)

Information on rural Peru	
People with clean water to drink	25%
People with proper sewage disposal	17%
1 in 5 children die from malnutrition and infectious diseases.	
There is poor farmland and so a very low standard of living.	
Rainfall in many areas is very low and unreliable.	
Most of the people are landless labourers.	

Reference Text Q4B

Self-help scheme A	Self-help scheme B
Provide workshops and training in every large village to make wind-powered pumps to bring water up from underground.	Provide health centres in every large village with one person in each village trained to treat common diseases and offer medical advice.

Look at Reference Texts Q4A and Q4B.

Reference Text Q4B describes two self-help schemes for improving conditions for people in rural Peru. The members of the Government cannot agree which is the better scheme. Describe the different points of view which they would put forward. (ES, 6)